Quoth The Raven, Veritas

Foreword

Chris Veritas began his alt media career quietly, with the creation of several websites dedicated to analyzing the subliminal occult meanings of various movies. Slowly, he moved into writing journalistic articles based on health, current events, and political philosophy. Toward the end of his life, his work turned more towards the spiritual aspects of both culture and politics as well as the relationship of humanity to its Creator. Eventually, poetry and spirituality were the final destinations of Chris Veritas the writer, right back where he started before the alt media ever heard his name. From poetry and songs to journalism, satire, and philosophy, back to poetry again.

In his short career as a writer, Chris Veritas produced an amazing body of work if not in quantity, certainly in quality. In the few articles Veritas wrote about American culture and the relationship of humanity to God and other humans, I couldn't help but feel a tinge of writer's jealousy. The ease in which he could communicate such massively important topics in a short concise essay in such a clear and relateable manner would make any writer wish he could master his own craft as Chris mastered his. His later philosophical work was the same. While many thinkers could fill volumes repeating questions and considerations making painfully detailed explanations as to why their narrow argument was correct, Chris' work would take up three pages of unassailable logic, three hundred pages swallowed up in concise wording, wittled down to a short perfectly flowing article.

Chris turned more to creative projects after he received the news of his terminal illness. He did express excitement at the idea of having a book put together of his journalistic and philosophical work and even took part in much of the organization and creative ideas behind this book as it stands. Unfortunately, Chris did not live to see the release of the book or the completion of the project. But that doesn't matter.

After the diagnosis, Chris turned more toward the spiritual in his work and in his life. Like his work, his life was short and, also like his work, though short, it was of the highest quality.

This book is barely a distinguishable fraction of who Chris Veritas was as a person but it was a part of him. It is my honor to have taken part in bringing it to a wider audience.

Brandon Turbeville

8/31/2017

TV and the Dark Powers That Be

Mediapharmaphilia is a neologism this journalist has invented to describe the complex relationship that exists between the Television user and his drug of choice; a dependency which leaves the poor addict dazzled and bedraggled; subjected to spectacle; and above all else, beholden to the Dealer for future installments of TERROR.

Like the erstwhile Media Sensation Patty Hearst, America has fallen in love with its captors, and seems to have come to expect the shock and awe and fear and trembling as a matter of course; except that it's not so much #ISIS that's delivering it. No, it's Wolf Shepherd and Blitzer O'reilly, our anchors in the restless sea of infinite (in)formation.

In the deep subconscious, which reassembles the dialectically opposed Network mirage, Wolf/Shepherd becomes both the guiding friend and the stern accuser, two voices that blend into one as the same source both defends and attacks Americans.

This dissonance I assert is designed to bypass and cripple the conscious mind, and the dirty little secret is this: we LOVE it. We are ALL Patty Hearst.

Yes, on some level we know all this, but we still won't stop watching. We stand by our Programming, and on any given day you might hear statements like these in defense of it: "You can't trust the MTV, but you can trust Wolf Shepherd"; I hate Barack Obama but, shh, let's hear what he has to say about Syria"; and "I'm terrified of ISEL™!; let's watch more San Bernardino coverage, post haste!".

It's all about trust. The public's potential distrust gets negated by a seemingly trustworthy alternative, in a neat shell game that keeps the Dark Forces just out of view, makes what's "cool" "hot", and being "down" with "what's up" a thing that's equal to your "level best"; unless of course things "go sideways".

Hey, Dark Forces, 1984 was not supposed to be an instruction manual [you Vampires].

But I digress.

As I speak the Telecaptors are, well, everywhere! They're in the McRonald's, at your doctor's office, your friendly neighborhood watering hole, and even at the café where I'm writing this article. It's just expected nowadays. The TV is a comforting presence that brings nostalgia with it. ("Know what I mean, Vern?")

It's the psychological crutch that fills the void of silence.

It's the Pavlovian bell that chimes to remind you of rendezvous with "Friends" (Sing it with me, N.B.C).

Speaking of friends, it's the new friend that's replaced intimacy, reading, and reasoned dialogue.

It's the wheel of discourse and supplier of water cooler punchlines; norms, fashions, and trends.

It's the subtle driving force generating consensus.

It's the fear that seeks nightmares, and the focus that blots out the external world.

It's an all-things-to-all-people reality machine and world-view supplier. (Wow, no wonder Allen Watt thinks it's weaponized).

In the movie "Gladiator", Russell Crowe's character, Maximus, pacing inside the bloody arena, shouts to the Romanized spectators, "Are you not entertained?". We have all been Romanized and brutalized by the Media's terrortainment. This united front would like us to accept as natural the presentation of Infinite Fear, interspersed with egregious "Two and a Half Men" episodes, and/or the latest BieberCyrusaur clone, purportedly "singing songs", and doing something that used to be called "dance". (But none of this is actually entertaining.)

Just where did the Beautiful and the Good disappear to, anyway? I lay this squarely at the feet of the Dark Powers That Be. Apparently Melody, Peace, and Harmony are not high priorities for them; and withdrawing these things without explanation, the gas lighting Media offers what's left to the willing captive, and Mediapharmaphilia ensues.

Brutalized, nadirized, and Wolf Shepherdized, the wary [yet trusting] American [captive] audience has fallen hard for its tormentor. Sometimes he wears a serious face, and sometimes a smirk of ironic detachment, but in all times and places he reminds of this poem which precedes the sad parable of the "Great Gatsby":

"Then wear the gold hat if that will move her;

If you can bounce high, bounce for her too,

Till she cry "lover, gold-hatted, high-bouncing lover,

I must have you!""

Threat Level Midnight

Yesterday president Obama appeared on television, and with as much gravity as the poor man could muster, once again reminded Americans not to forget about TERROR! (Gee, thanks. I had almost forgotten for a minute.)

Whatever happened to the iconic FDR who stood before an uncertain world and said, "The only thing we have to fear is fear itself"?

Obama spoke from the headquarters of some alphabet agency I've never heard of, on the same day it was announced that things said on Social Media "may" soon factor-in to the acquisition of passports. (Hope you kept your trap shut.) And just like that, there goes your Freedom of Speech.

Think of all the ways speech gets limited these days. A host of alphabet Networks and Agencies spells it all out for the public. We have to watch what we say due to political correctness, use words and phrases that are fashionable and avoid those that are passé, and speak what is acceptable as discourse and eschew what is restricted. And now unpopular speech is to be punished by the restricting of Liberties?

Oh, excuse me; that's only for the "terrorists".

It's a shame the American people haven't yet figured out that the terrorists were created by the (by now obviously) corrupted Western Governments, in order ultimately to scare the public into giving up its rights. And although this may be evident, the excuses given by Big Media are so pervasive and compelling! Here is a sampling: "We have to limit Freedoms so that the terrorists won't win." "The terrorists envy us our rights, so we have to give up our rights in order to secure them." "The only way we can be at peace is to constantly be at war." "War is peace." (And by the way, did you hear, "We've always been at war with Eurasia?".)

Once you realize that the Evil Western Powers are parasitically preying on their own peoples, it begins to make sense why all of a sudden shooters of all stripes are coming out of the woodwork, in an entirely new sociological phenomena; becoming, each, the poster boy for a different political agenda. Then and only then will you understand that the #alQaedIsis State is but a Western Brand for terror, just like your friendly neighborhood Wendy's is a Brand for hamburgers.

When you start to grasp the narrative of the war on Freedom; pardon me, terror; the absurdity of the Televised Drama becomes bracingly clear. Then you can take back your peace by laughing at these tyrants like the Founders would have, by mocking them, by comparing their two-bit, tinhorn soap opera to such ludicrous fare as Michael Scott's fictional self-made "Office" movie, "Threat Level Midnight", a hilarious title which seems to spoof the post-9/11 "Color Alert" boondoggle, and the sangfroid Cold War "Dooms Day Clock".

Itself a spoof of life in the age of terrorism (and of Bond films), "Threat Level Midnight" features a terror-loving double crosser of a president, an outrageous cartoon villain, a robot butler who might as well represent England, and a dopey hero who doesn't even know he's a joke. Voila, the war on terror, 2015! (I don't even have to break this down, do I?)

To some it may seem like escapism, but in an age where the president pops in just to remind you to crap your pants, I prefer to watch a fictional president betray his country. Hey, at least everyone knows *that guy* is an actor.

So like Webster Tarpley, who may or may not be making fun of Obama when he calls him "Obammer", let's take a deep breath and remember that life is full of beauty and non-political thrills. And in any case, "blessed are the peacemakers", and "blessed are the merciful"; and those that "hunger and thirst for righteousness" (we must believe it) will one day "inherit the earth".

Let's remember this Christmas season to remain in a spirit of joy and peace; this is how we break the War Machine, and confound the Media Industrial Complex.

Three Cheers For The War Machine

Did you know the Pentagon pays millions to the NFL to display "earnest and heartfelt patriotism"? Well, not anymore, since word got out. That means all the giant flags unfurled over fields, and the F-16's screaming overhead, were not displayed out of love for country. But I bet most thought they were.

These days in America it's all about war. Big Media harps endlessly about it, civilians are wearing camouflage as a fashion statement, the Middle East is on everybody's lips, and being pro-war is the only position one dares to profess ("*You* don't support *terrorism*, do you?").

Indeed, today it is very popular to be a war-hawk: to want to bomb Syria, the Islamic State (wherever that is), and hey, why not bomb Russia while we're at it? (Syria is right on their doorstep, strangely enough).

But America's long history of dubious foreign entanglements, which are always procured by Big Media, ought to make us slow to trust new operations and believe the public justifications for them. And we would be, too, except that we can't remember the past.

Former president Eisenhower was the ultimate insider, and he warned us as far back as the 1950's that, after seeing with his own eyes where the War Machine was heading, America had better "beware the military industrial complex"; that is, the system that makes weapons for profit, and needs wars to justify its existence.

"But aren't we making the world safe for Democracy", you might ask? Truly, we have to get past such simplistic thinking and start to grasp realpolitik, a term which means that power is the driving factor in decision making in the Real World. The first step is to realize we have been lied to about almost everything regarding politics, and especially regarding war. (But this is not surprising, given that Democracies have a shelf life of only about 200 years. After this, the leadership becomes corrupt. Does this come as a surprise?)

Here are a few examples of the boondoggles that have been brought to us by the War Machine, and its partner in crime, the Media Industrial Complex.

1: By now everyone should know we overthrew the Persian Government in 1953 because of oil, changing the course of history for that nation forever, and preparing the way for the Ayatollah, tons of terrorism, and decades of international friction which persists to this day. Have we ever acknowledged this? Is there any indication that this taints our ability to wage just wars?

2: Next, we trained and armed the Mujahedeen in Afghanistan and they became al Qaeda and the Taliban. This is flat out embarrassing, if not obliquely nefarious.

3: Moving sequentially, let's be sure to remember how the Reagan Administration sold weapons to Iran to fund the Contras. Wait, I thought Iran was the enemy?

4: Speaking of enemies, why isn't Saudi Arabia an enemy, when they practically personify the spirit of Jihad? Nope. They're our trusted ally in the war against humanity. Excuse me, extremism.

And now it's come to the surface from Hillary's emails that the State Department and a coterie of Slick Hilly's compadres trained and armed terrorists in Libya, to funnel them into Syria, in order to overthrow Assad. (Wait; excuse me, "ISIS".) I don't imagine it was White House bureaucrats who taught them how to fight, however; eh, John McCain?

We've bombed Syrian universities and hospitals, displaced 60% of the population, and caused an enormous refugee crisis. This is after turning Afghanistan, Iraq and Libya into replicas of the surface of the

Moon. Perhaps the Pentagon wants to see how large a crater it can create? If so, they're off to a good start.

Then there is the crater Big Media has left in the American intellect, obscuring memory and cognitive function. Certain camps attribute psychological warfare to the Media, which might explain the constant bombardment with fear, explosive news, and shell-shocking terror coverage.

In this school of thought, Big Media is the true terrorist.

Should, then, the Media be trusted when it comes to compelling war, when it seems to lie constantly and egregiously, as it sets the stage for an environment where the Machine can sell weapons, profit mightily, and make the public pay for the privilege? And should we not take the war-making privilege away from the Vampires who profit from bloodshed?

Sun Tzu explained centuries ago that you can't keep fighting wars forever, if you don't want your country to fall apart. (Unless, of course, that is your actual objective.)

But an even greater Sage once solemnly declared, "He who lives by the sword, dies by the sword", then he reached down to heal the wound of His enemy.

Beware The Media Industrial Complex

In conversations with various people, I have often brought up the fact that the Media seems to have no memory of the past, is entirely uniform when it comes to urging war, and patently ignores a plethora of glaring issues. The issues it does catch sight of, it seems incapable of penetrating, remaining at the surface of things, and therefore keeping discourse at the most superficial level.

When questioned about these tendencies of Media, the responses I've received range from "well, that's just the way they maintain ratings", to "but my paper or network has the better ideology". Americans appear satisfied to accept what occurs to them as given, and like Pangloss to reply, indeed, this is "the best of all possible worlds".

I beg to differ.

Here are a few troubling questions that I feel greatly undermine the idea that Main Stream Media is credible:

1: Why is it that when it comes to war, the same news sources that criticize the president constantly, suddenly all seem to lionize his cause? Shouldn't the opposite be true? Shouldn't there be at least some dissent among the Main Stream sources? Isn't this a little suspicious, if the press is free and independent?

2: How can it be that not only the press, but the entire nation has forgotten that the first case made to the American people concerning war with Syria was sold as being in order to depose Assad? Clearly ISIS existed at that point, so why were they not the target? When exactly did they become the world's Super Enemy? Apparently this happened a few months after the Media campaign to attack Syria by other means failed.

3: When did it become okay to terrorize the viewing audience, weaving dubious tales of extremists hiding under every bush, meanwhile replaying distressing footage over and over again (like the falling of the towers), until the public is thoroughly brutalized? How many times did we need to see the towers fall? 1,000? 10,000? How disrespectful to the dead, and to the living.

4: When exactly did the trail of bodies following the Clintons not become news anymore?

Questions, questions, questions. And these are just the tip of the iceberg.

With a bit of research it becomes apparent that the entire Media apparatus is beholden to a handful of enormously powerful Corporations, which teach the public that this, of course, is a good thing. Corporations ought to be as large as possible they say, because: Capitalism! If the prevailing ideology makes them insanely powerful, and "accidentally" coincides with 99% of Americans being poor and in debt, well, at least we're not Communists!

And that is what you call a false dialectic.

These entities therefore, through their Media medium, construct opinion, polarize politics, shred the past like Winston in 1984, and obscure the present with the dope of hypnotic flicker rates, tantalizing tag lines, and the literal dope of drugs like Prozac and Ritalin, a la Brave New World.

But what would a legitimate media look like, you might ask?

1: A legitimate media would harp incessantly on our nation's constant violation of international law when waging war, and the hypocrisy of claiming to defend Democracy while violating it.

2: A legitimate media would remember that the Fed promised before its inception to scientifically prevent booms and busts, inflation, depressions, and crashes. Rather than analyze its promises and policies, what we get is stale superficial commentary, which completely overlooks history and current reality. No one apparently can criticize the printing of endless paper money, the mountains of debt our economy runs on, or the international banks (of which the Fed is one), which strip countries bare of resources (see: North America), and gamble trillions on derivatives while forcing austerity onto entire nations. And all the economists can say is: "wow, look at those fourth quarter gains".

3: A legitimate media would run Trump and Hillary straight into the Gulf, and refuse to ratify the side show spectacle of our so-called presidential electoral proceedings.

Amidst the glossy blues and reds of our dynamic digital cable displays (which seem to progress faster than the state of politics), planes are disappearing and we're chasing pings, North Korea is hacking Sony in a fit of pique, Bill O'reilly is killing great men faster than you can say "obstreperous", while talking heads yell talking points on split screens to a divided audience.

Is this "just the way things are", or are we being gamed?

To many, it is becoming clear that the Media is now an organized apologetics machine, and is no longer a source for information, as it pours forth the dialectics of the Anglo-American establishment. Big Money, which owns Big Media, supersizes the insignificant; barricades inconvenient facts; sells politics like Big Macs; tempts cravenly the debt-ridden with overpriced expendables; is tre cool with hyping vacuous celebrities, one note politicians and golden doors, all at one time and with great gusto.

And we become dumber and dumber as we absorb it all: fake news, fake money, fake culture, and fake representative Government. (Ah, America in 2015. Each day is better than the next.)

Former president Eisenhower once famously said, "Beware the military industrial complex", and we should have listened to him. But now the objectives of Big Military, Big Media/ Business/ Entertainment, and Big White House all seamlessly merge and overlap. One could be excused for wondering if we're living in a thinly disguised tyranny, when the light of truth seems so strictly verboten.

Killing The Culture Of Death

On radio, iTunes, and MTV the Stars are aligned, singing "Die Young" and "Born to Die".

A former Poison Giant now supplies a large portion of the nation's food supply, and a mega Soda Corp. uses fetal stem-cells in the lab to "enhance flavor".

Meanwhile Government subsidizes the clinical elimination of millions of unborn children, as Media collectively makes marriage appear absurd and/or impossible, and child-rearing unappealing drudgery. But eternal narcissism and categorical infertility (pardon my French, "la joie de vie"), are made to look as alluring as the golden apple Eris threw in-between Hera and Aphrodite at the wedding which caused the Trojan War. (Poor Paris, he didn't stand a chance.)

Alas, Big Money has its paw-prints all over this mess: the same Cabal that lurks behind Big Media, running roughshod over the rubrics of life, the cause of confabulation in the minds of Americans. Furthermore, due to its immensity, said Cabal is able to use the intricate machinery of Institutions and Corporations like a virus uses the organelles of a host cell.

The proceeding nonsense is brought to you by the SIX death-dealing Corporations that own the entire Media:

1: The slick advertising campaigns that sell the endless wars (hats off, seriously, for somehow getting away with having no debates at all. I'm totally impressed, Oligarchs);

2: The Entertainment Mainstream's fascination with Witchcraft and Sorcery, with good old family Disney being a prime proponent ("Charmed", I'm sure);

3: The nearly infinite permutations of the Zombie theme (or perhaps you didn't notice);

4: The ubiquitous Ghost Shows, with (of course!) a corresponding Medium trudging through the haunting;

5: the suavely construed sex and death confections (even I felt a little tug for Santa Muerte while watching Bond with his lady friend during "SPECTRE's" festival scene);

6: And just because there ought to be six examples, how about the deadly pills the TV pushes that can potentially kill, but are sold with glossy butterflies and smiling pill-poppers?

This is by no means an exhaustive list.

The point I'm trying to make is that Television and Media are the chief propagandists and apologists for the Culture Death. Go ahead, try and find a Mainstream source that's wholesome and in the service of life (take your time, I'll wait); or a Government, for that matter! Sure, there is the "Hallmark Channel", which tries to affect that "greeting card feel", but even they tend to run shows that disempower women. In fact, "Hallmark" is a good example for citing a trend: with all Media, it seems a small of amount of the displaying of the Good builds up a certain level of trust, which is followed by countless examples of lies, betrayals, and sex and death all intertwined.

It's no stretch to see that in one way or another, the entirety of Big Money/Media seems allied against fertility, family, and the life of Western Culture; selling happiness as the ultimate objective, while honors, riches, and pleasures supersede child-bearing and family continuity, which (please take note) seem actually to lead to a next generation.

But someone will say, "Yeah, well that's just done for copy". Okay, still not convinced?

Then consider how society's "vaunted humanitarians", Bill and Melinda Gates, have been seeking to extend the future of Africa: by handing out *condoms and birth control*. (Hey, who needs fresh water and agriculture, anyway?). Next, add in the supra-national "animals first, earth first, humans are a scourge" "Green Movement" into the mix. And please remember that the "Green-Gates" of Big Philanthropy inevitably open onto the dark frontiers of Big Money.

Still another person will say, "That? That's all just accidental"; or, "Nothing could be so organized. How could televised zombies, endless wars, a supposed infertility agenda, and the Green Movement all factor into one ultra-organized culture of death?".

I hear you, but I would point out to that person they need to research the Council of 300, the Bilderberger Group, and, for good measure, check out John Rappaport's work on the Trilateral Commission. Seriously, these cats are organized, supremely powerful, and corrupt beyond description.

It is just such societies as ours that, having become rationalistic, mechanistic, and supremely powerful, with the full force of cynicism, begin to attack life while overdosing on pleasure. A good historical touchstone would be Carthage. With its vast trading capability and unrivaled wealth, like us, it became a culture obsessed with death, and sought to subdue the world while incinerating its own children. So too with the Aztecs, who sacrificed the living at the service of material ends, and played games that they imagined had eternal consequences. In short, materialism makes society inverted, and therefore insane.

These tendencies are almost exclusively the fruit of ossified societies, like our own; only, our society has become part of a world civilization, and thus the threat is extended to all humanity. So if you are still wondering why the elite should create such a culture, perhaps the better observation would be to realize that it is such a culture that has created them.

On the surface, everything from death-dealing cancer care, to the free and Democratic progression of Euthanasia, may seem random and innocuous. If so, that's actually scarier to me than a conspiracy, because that kind of "random" uniformity may actually suggest some form of spiritual warfare.

Many researchers will tell you that as you ascend to the summits of Power, Money, and Control, the price of admission becomes an allegiance to Darkness. And this particular journalist believes the Dark Powers That Be are nearing an organized endgame scenario. After all, how much bigger and more powerful do their Institutions need to become, before they finally tighten the noose, or perhaps simply collapse it all?

But whether satanic or simply spiteful, when you view the scene from above, it appears the Dark Powers are hell bent on destroying the Beautiful, the Good, and the life of the world.

It is my contention that all the aforementioned is intentional; that, impossible as this may sound, it is a complex international operation; and that there is most likely a spiritual aspect at work, as well.

Unfortunately for the Dark Powers, as any well-read child can tell you, there is an "Ancient Magic" (in the words of C.S. Lewis) that has always brought life out of death. And if you doubt it, just try and figure out how life came into existence from nothingness and persists despite all obstacles.

All the gnostic hatred leveled by Darkness at the Source of Life must necessarily destroy itself by itself, because destruction is the only thing Death really knows how to do.

The bigger they are, the harder they fall.

Take that, Dark Powers.

The Croc Obama

Barack Obama is such a softie. He just cries and cries, his heart is THAT BIG.

When I hear people criticizing the president, I think of the wonder of Obamacare, that unique piece of "legislation" that was never Congressionally ratified, but still became Law; and of Gaymarriagecare, which was never Congressionally ratified, but still became Law; and most recently of Gunbackgroundcheckcare, which may never be ratified, but… well, you get the idea.

Standing before the nation this Tuesday, weeping like a saltwater crocodile, Mr. Obama revealed yet another Executive Order to the people; ostensibly conceived as a quick response to gun violence. And before you could say "Fast and Furious", with his copious tears he had washed away all memory of Checks and Balances. (But as to deaths due to bombs and drones, his eyes betrayed no sign of recognition.)

Immediately following the press conference, Big Media went into hyper-drive, praising the president for his "emotional response", but declaring his measures sadly unsatisfactory. "Can't we have Orwellian legislation that's more Draconian", said the New York Times and CNN, "for the children's sake? We must gut the Constitution to protect the people from Lawlessness!"

Little did Big Media seem to notice, but by bypassing Congressional voting on such a grand scale, the Constitutional Lawyer in Chief and his coterie of High Court Judges have effectively eclipsed public representation, which is essentially The People itself. What a crock!

Everywhere you look, Barack Obama is caring Democracy into oblivion.

Here are a few examples:

1: By caring for public health, he's destroying health care and small business.

2: By caring for gay rights, he's made the states impotent to determine their own fates regarding non-enumerated issues.

3: By caring for races, he's run them right into the ground.

4: By caring for security, he's turned George Orwell into a prophet.

5: And because of his love for Marxist politics; wait, excuse me, the Democratic Platform; Mr. Crocodile Tears has given us a tutorial on clever destabilization campaigns.

These campaigns have been run against Americans, by Obama, from his very emergence. The first campaign manifested itself as a typical "color revolution", which placed the requisite signs into ecstatic hands, with the usual one word slogan and color pattern, to boot. In this case the word read "change". "Change", eh? Did anybody think to ask what that change would entail? Who could have guessed it would have meant the change from a Democratic Republic to a Federal Tyranny?!

(Perhaps you think it extreme to call what we have today a tyranny? Well, what else would you call a Government that bypasses the people, in violation of its charter? Go ahead and think, I have time to wait...)

Beyond his initial entry into politics, the President has been very busy destabilizing society using the usual Marxist bag of tricks; pitting men against women, gays against straights, blacks against whites, rich against poor, and US versus THEM. But I can already hear the objection; "Hey, that's just Democratic politics, compassion and progress." To that objection I would like to once again say, "what a crock!" That is not politics, that's the Communist Manifesto.

Having said all that, my question is this: are we just going to accept what The Croc is doing and has done? The Media seems perfectly happy to accept it, and the bypassed impotents (that is, Congress) affect a similar reaction. In fact, Congress seems perfectly happy with the status quo, so long as the quid pro quo flows, and the dubious treaties fly. And Media just sighs and moves on to the next topic.

Now the Courts are legislating, the White House is weeping, Congress is sleeping, the Media is pointing fingers, and politicians are prancing and blabbing; while Americans are texting and snickering, Twittering and purchasing caffeinated brew. So please tell me, who exactly is manning the switch?

In my mind, all this apparent chaos has a clear pattern, and the key to it is understanding that destabilization is the desired outcome, not an accidental occurrence. For President Marx and his band of culture warriors, the State must reign supreme, and all manner of feigning is licit in the attainment of this goal. After all, what are the people compared to the supereminent state? But of course the people must be fooled and outmaneuvered, and this can only be done by outfoxing them, and tricking them into sympathizing.

Thus Obama's strange hobby horse; the employment of subterfuge in the form of pretended care, to reduce the American people to irrelevance. It's really a very neat trick. (But not as neat a trick as teaching a reptile how to cry. *That* is a stroke of genius.)

Representing Big Marxism and Big Federalism, The Croc Obama, Constitutional Lawyer extraordinaire, seems content to serve up tyranny with methodical pathos, affecting either ironic detachment or weepy sentimentality, according to the needs of the given day.

Somebody give this man an Oscar, and whisk him off the stage with a giant cane.

The Paradox That Trumps The Donald

These days, it's all pretty much bad news. Bad news is HUGE.

Strangely enough, in a time when everything seems wrong with the world, Donald Trump becomes, perhaps, the right man for the times. This statement may make little sense on the face of it, but reality is full of paradoxes. Therefore, allow me a bit of leeway to make my case. Let's begin by setting the stage for the environment he is moving about in; an environment which I believe he personifies, and whose starkness his antics illuminate.

First of all, let's examine the Chinese stock market, which kept getting shut down this week because the Yuan had a yen for jagging. (Good thing the markets aren't interconnected.) You'd think that after 2,000 years of Buddhism, they would have figured out how karma works, vis a vis their recent currency devaluations. On the other hand, this may eventually help them sink the Island of Taiwan, if they don't sink their own continent first.

More emails from Slick Hilly have now been released, with Big Media focusing like lasers on the most important aspects, such as: "who did Hillary dine with"; "what did they talk about"; and "what did they have for dessert"? Meanwhile, less important fare, like al Qaeda's infiltration among our beloved moderate rebels; Libya's billions in gold that went, um, where?; and the now debunked story of Gaddafi and the weaponized Viagra, was also revealed, but fortunately slipped by our Media gatekeepers. Honestly, the truth is just too messy for prime-time. We now return to our regularly scheduled program, brought to you by Cialis.

And speaking of debunked stories, did you hear that a UN weapons expert, a Ms. Carla Del Ponte, has stated that President Assad did not gas his own people, but that our beloved moderate rebels did? Nope, neither did I. Not from any main stream news source, at least.

And before we move on, let's remember how the War Machine is turning the Levant into a giant crater, while at home, we're being cleverly disarmed. How's that for imports/exports, Mr. Art Vandelay?

To resurrect our refrain, as we all feel and know, pretty much everything seems wrong with the world; which is why Donald Trump is the right man for the times. Not that he's a good candidate, per se; it's more that he personifies the spirit of the world today, and the current problems facing America. As such, his presence is instructional and could serve as a wake-up call.

In what ways does Donald Trump represent today's America? Here are a few
examples:

1: He's rich, and yet entirely bankrupt as a leading figure. (Compare that with Tax Revenue/Government debt.) Plus, just as he has made billions by inflating his name as a brand, so has the Treasury made billions (out of thin air) by inflating the dollar. In both cases, a few men have profited, but the majority feels the effects of disparity's diminishing returns.

2: He's bellicose, and attacks at random. And just as our military claims to invade countries for the sake of Democracy, Trump claims to fire shots at his opponents in defense of the Republic. But just as American bombs tend to hit civilian targets like schools and hospitals, so his invective strikes such innocents as the Mexican people, the Muslim people, the Syrian people, moderators like Megyn Kelly, and erstwhile celebrities like Rosie O'Donnell.

3: He's HUGE, just like the American economy. And like said economy, he tends to go bust from time to time.

4: And he represents our Infotainment culture; a strange reality hybrid, which mistakes his sound bites for a campaign platform. For example, unlike JFK, who challenged us to fly to the moon, Trump exclaims, "bang, zoom, to the moon"; next, rather than propose breaking down barriers between peoples and nations, he declares a Great Wall should be built on the southern border, with some weird "golden door"; and rather than heightening public discourse, he merely raises the decibel level; which in a sense does amplify discussion (in the way that a megaphone amplifies a jackhammer).

For all these reasons, Donald Trump is the right man to run against the Left; as long as we find Obama disarming, and Hillary as transparent as white-water.

Until we are able to be a cogent, disciplined people, who prefer reasoned dialogue to inflammatory rhetoric; peace to war; real news sources to those that prestidigitate; and well-rounded world-views, as opposed to those categorically set against the East; then, perhaps, the Trumps of the world may well serve as the instructive personifications we need. As such, they "hold a mirror up to nature", so we may fully see ourselves.

It's strange how international intrigue spills over and affects nations half a world away; economic instability is now a quotidian reality; and what was written in the dark by a stark force of nature has become a reality broadcast from the rooftops. And then, to top it all off, this wild international backdrop becomes the natural setting for two fronts to collide and resolve themselves.

This is the silver lining in the coming showdown, as America witnesses the Brash Windbag take on the Dark Tornado.

On Voting For the Lesser of Two Evils

In this stark political landscape, I seem to find myself caught between Scylla and Charybdis; between the devil and the deep blue sea, vis-à-vis the future of the country; given the apparent void among viable presidential candidates.

"A void", you might say; "aren't there actually too many?"

Well, yes; in the way that there are perhaps too many types of fast food restaurants; but no-one would accuse them of being nourishing.

When I think of the desperate shape our country is in, and its desperate need for not good, but great leadership; and I see on one side perhaps the worst political candidate ever; versus a veritable smorgasbord of Jordan Bakers, Tom Buchanans, and Meyer Wolfsheims; I must admit, my first inclination is to write the entire system off as being unworthy of participation.

To top it all off, none of the candidates, Republican or Democrat, are coming to us with platforms that suit reality. Instead, discounting Trump's mania, they are merely towing the line of their parties; dragging along the dross of old stances and traditional nostalgia. Even the Democrats prove regressive in their predictable progressive stance.

Should I vote for one of the War-Hawk Republicans, simply to oppose Slick Hilly? When push comes to shove, do I actually believe in the lesser of two evils mentality? Would a Ted Cruz or a Marco Rubio really be better? After all, with a Republican comes all the baggage of the Neo-con Right; The Pentagon; and the Corporate Super-Conglomerators.

Let's be clear, realpolitik is reality; and a modern president now represents a whole host of entrenched interests, which wield power like

Oligarchs. Whether it be the Pentagon, the CIA, or the Federal Reserve, he puts a face on all these enormous, abstract entities, providing the illusion of continuity of Government. They existed before him, they will exist after him; and year by year they grow and increase in power, like little monarchies within the free Democratic state.

Which Hillary alternative has spoken a word about the deeper problems facing America? Like our inverted birth pyramid; the derivatives nightmare; our hypocritical foreign alliances; or the Media's facts-amnesia? And who could do so and still remain a candidate?

Questions, questions, questions; and each one is more troubling than the last.

And yet, there is still Hillary Clinton, who is clearly a grave, grave danger to freedom and all forms of life. It is really astonishing how she has becomes the personification of the spirit of incorporation; though she pretends to represent "ordinary Americans". From her work at Wal-Mart, antagonizing their labor force; to her nearly umbilical ties to Big Money and Big Warfare, this Wall Street War-Hawk rides high on a sea of green, stuffing her pockets for cheap political access. (Seriously, how does she get away with it, magic?)

And then there is the troubling fact that people close to her keep dying.

But is the matter grave enough to vote for the likes of a Donald Trump, should he (God forbid!) receive the Republican nomination? He is really awful, but probably not as awful as Hillary; so, is the lesser evil a better evil, if only so by one degree?

Have we really come to the point where we are voting for an evil, to stop an evil, in order to produce some sort of good?

Would it be better to say no to the voting process all together, or to fight the danger imperfectly; perhaps incurring deep responsibility for the deaths of foreign human beings, our brothers and sisters, who will inevitably fall victim to the Military Industrial Complex's greed and ambivalence toward life?

These questions trouble me in the way they resist resolution; and I admit I don't have the answers; as I stand between Scylla and Charybdis, staring at both beasts, wondering which one to slay.

On Man As A Transcendent Being

"What a piece of work is a man! How noble in reason, how infinite in faculty! In form and moving how express and admirable! In action how like an angel, in apprehension how like a god!"

In a world seemingly become bereft of the transcendent, what is the true measure of a man? And what is it that makes a man fully human? Is he as "admirable" as Hamlet asserts, as he compares man to an "angel" and "a god"? And how strange that this same "paragon" provides him no "delight"; for, in the play, man uses his "noble reason" merely to execute base material actions.

Is the purpose of man to aspire to be angelic, or does he exist to serve the State, the Corporation, and the Economic Engine, as the ancients believed? And if the answer to the latter question is yes, should those who are found burdensome not be eliminated? I ask because the ancients believed that, also, and it seems we are heading in that direction once again.

For today's world, which has returned to a materialist conception, it's important to point out there is a 1 to 1 ratio between the veneration of the imminent, and the reducing of human beings to mere objects and/or obstacles.

Backtracking a few millennia, Seneca, the Stoic philosopher, left to posterity a detailed record of the Roman practice of infanticide. The utility of such an action is clear enough, and was considered laudable to the Roman world, which saw human beings as being mere material objects. Not to be outdone, the vaunted Greek philosopher, Plato, argued for the elimination of "useless old men". These two were among the greatest minds the ancient world ever produced, and they both favored doing away with the weak.

But after Christ, it was as if the world were split in two.

Spiritual reasoning raised the status of individuals above the all-powerful monolithic State, because after Christ it began to be acknowledged that human beings have immortal souls. Only spirit has true value; and we demonstrate our belief in this by how we treat animals. If we stop believing in spirit, we stop revering human life; and the revolution in human values is finished.

Paradoxically, this window into intangible eternity is what makes visible individuals count in reality; a thing like hope, tenable; and blind faith, sensible. On the face of it, it makes no sense that this should be the case; but with human beings, the supernatural tends to explain us better than anything else.

To hope is not rational in the same way an algebraic equation is; yet it is fitting for a creature that cannot be explained perfectly according to utility. Unreasonable hope advances life in the face of impossible odds, and is therefore perfectly practical. Blind faith leads men to cherish things that cannot be seen, but ends by enhancing the world of visible objects.

Most men don't dream corporate dreams, or have reveries of working on assembly lines; but they do dream of the music of Mozart, the art of geniuses like Fra Angelico, and of the joys of family life.

These things make no sense, really; after all, what have they to do with survival, production, or progress? But the truth is, our deepest desires are spiritual, even if we think we are only animal.

Now, you may object, "I don't see Honey Boo-Boo listening to Mozart".

Poor Honey Boo-Boo. She is the perfect example of what can happen when the question "what is the true measure of a man" is neglected.

Building on this, when man cherishes the Invisible, and looks with respect on supernal Eminence, it is a powerful incentive to infuse excellence into what is imminent.

When human beings abandon this principle, in favor of a material view, then they abandon transcendence; which is intricately tied to the sanctity of life. Thus today's rampant abortions; objectifying pornography; infinite imprisonment; trash TV and degrading reality culture; and the odd absurdity of corporations becoming people, while people become the problem of statisticians.

For the modern world, it really *is* people that are the problem (although, all is well if you're a Future or a Currency). Apparently, there are too many of us, especially in places where they can't afford to buy Big Macs (like Africa); or are too old to flip them (like the Netherlands).

Societies that deal exclusively in trade or conquest (or both), exhaust human transcendence, which ought to be considered a human right. A life lived on the treadmill ignores the unrepeatable artist in the man, who becomes subject to the endless repetition of a lifeless product.

But when the same man is allowed to create, watch as he begins to crystallize some unknown aspect of eternity into an object, in the effort to still time, and enjoy some measure of Heaven. (This may not line a man's pockets, but does man exist for money's sake?)

Transcendence means that this sort of mechanization just doesn't suit humanity, strange creatures that we are. Anything less than deep reverence for the Invisible makes us lower than the objects beneath us; but when we long for the Good with hope, only then do we begin to resemble the Image of our invisible Creator.

Indeed, our transcendence is a paradox, because what makes us fully human is our immaterial spirit. The flesh is of no avail.

Now, if we could just get Honey Boo-Boo on board. That, too, would be a paradox; for the first time, a drone turning into a Queen.

On the Spirit of Rights, and Remaking the World

In this day and age, where confusion is rampant, and the inversion of American Principles a thoroughgoing affair, I think it crucial to renew knowledge of the origin of our Rights and Freedoms, that we may the better defend them from their most subtle enemies.

It's an open secret that the Declaration declares the Rights of Americans to be the gift of God, not the gift of Government; which turns said gift into grift. As such, they are not magnanimous largesse, similar to a welfare check or entitlement; but something "inalienable"; which, essentially, means Government derives its power from free persons who "consent" to be governed, and not the other way 'round.

You wouldn't think this is the case, the way the President behaves, and the Courts legislate; as they bypass the people, to push controversial or unpassable policy. (Hey, what ever happened to Sic Semper Tyrannis?)

If the Obama Administration had its way, the revolution in human values would be over.

Extremely telling was the President's speech, on the day when he declared the Beatitudes to be dangerous to Liberty. Either he doesn't understand that this is where the idea of individual Liberty came from; or he does, and he was mounting an indirect assault at it. And frankly, I can't say which is worse.

Let's backtrack a moment. Before the Beatitudes, before Christ, there was the pagan world, which had Rome as its shining pinnacle. Though containing laws and a complex legal code, Rome was extremely venal; and the rich and powerful were favored, while the poor and unconnected were considered expendable. (Sound familiar?) In short, the

State was the true living being, and "goddess Rome", and "divine Caesar", alone, had transcendent importance.

What was the meaning of one human life? A man lived and died, and nothing remained of him. At best, he might be remembered as a hero, and thus obtain some measure of immortality. *Perhaps* for the powerful, the case could be different; if the inscrutable gods were impressed with their prowess. But for ordinary men, there was no eternal life; and thus, no fraternal Rights.

But everything changed after Christ.

Although He was not actively teaching political theory, His ideas still revolutionized the way human beings saw Themselves and their States.

The foundation of this revolution is the idea that all human beings have Spirits, which make them eternal; and, therefore, invaluable. Governments will pass away; stars will pass away; the universe will cease to be; but even the least among humanity will outlive the universe, the stars, and the might of "divine Caesar".

The true spirit of the revolution in Rights is the revelation that Spirit alone gives value to life. (Not that the animals are valueless; in fact, the more spiritual a person is, the more they will tend to care for lesser beings.)

Now, the values of the Spirit are the values of the "peacemaker"; the "meek"; and the "poor in spirit"; that is, those who are not unnaturally attached to riches and power. Not that riches and power are always evils, but they do tend to become inimical to individuals; especially as States advance and become ossified. You will, of course, recognize the Beatitudes, here; but perhaps you didn't realize how dangerous they are to the Barack Obamas of the world, or how essential to modern Democracies?

Unlike the way the ancients practiced Democracy (which, in truth, was very little different from a suffragettic Oligarchy), we practice it as an inherently free; voluntarily peaceful; valued citizenry; mostly composed of – get this – ordinary workers! (that is, the "meek"). Truly, the Founders got it right when they linked human Rights to God, because only a God could guarantee the cause of the powerless in this cruel world.

Super Corporatization, Federalization, and all the enormous "isms" of modernity, are like armed men hired out against the individual; and the "subtle" societal campaigns against religion (affecting superiority in the name of Rights), are like a steep road leading us right back to Rome.

To avoid this potentiality, the human Spirit must be held eternal and priceless; this alone places the State beneath our feet.

Otherwise, peoples tend to end up subject to "geniuses" like Marx and Lenin; two materialists who thought their type of State to be the "final revolution" in the history of humanity. (Of course, their "brilliant insights" led to the deaths of nearly 100 million people.) Not to reduce all opposition to a straw man, but it seems the contact of modern, spiritually enlightened Democracies, with atheistic counter-movements, has produced nothing but slaughters.

(Sorry, Karly; the revolution is not of this world.)

Human beings are always trying to create utopias. Regardless of this, I imagine there will continue to be tension between the poor and the rich; Peoples and States; and Spirit and material. This dynamic tension has the power to produce wonders for the world; or make miserable environments, like the Gulag Archipelago.

You see, in the midst of all this tension, it's clear; we can have whatever we want, now. Our eyes have been opened by a new tree and a new fruit. The old world had gone as far as it could; but in the new, the eternal opens out before human beings, once again.

At this crucial moment, let's be clear; the source of human Rights is not to be found in institutions; politicians; or manifestoes. No; it's in a blazing Concept, Supernal and Spiritual.

This Perfections seems to be the final purpose of man; a creature with *such enormous potential* for the Beautiful and the Good.

God-willing, he will wake up and realize who he really is; and remake the world in the spirit of his true Image and Likeness.

On Evolution As The Assassin's Arrow

It appears to me there is a direct connection between all things Darwinian, and the degeneration of modern life and culture; as Darwin's theory of evolution has taken the once Transcendent heart of man, and left it effectively shipwrecked on the shores of the Galapagos. Quite the paradox, isn't it, that a theory claiming the existence of evolution should produce the opposite result?

While said evolution claims to situate life, and put truth in its proper place, in actuality, it really works against both. First of all, it does this by being a theory masquerading as fact; second, by existing and predominating without evidence; and third, by dangerously inverting essential human ideals and necessities.

The peril of the first two examples ought to be obvious enough, though I don't see many challenging them. I find this truly bizarre. After all, isn't the scientific system supposed to test hypotheses and verify their truthfulness? Not here, ladies and gentleman. Here you will only find dogmatism, and a blind faith in what must be, rather than what is confirmed by evidence. (Wait, I thought dogma only belonged in Churches?) In short, the systematic promulgation of theories as facts ought to make everyone shudder.

But as to the third example, it turns out to be much more dangerous; because the tenets of Darwinism aim right at the source of meaning, in the minds of men.

Meaning, the mind is a machine that runs on meaning. Now, by turning man into an accident, Darwin and his proteges have unwittingly struck at the very fabric of the mind, itself. For if this mind, which innately classifies each thing according to its essence, thinks itself to be without purpose, then the result must needs be despair, and/or relativism.

What does despair lead to but death and destruction? What has the twentieth century been filled with but these same things? What has been our prevailing theory on life and progress during that time? The answer, of course, is that we have bought into a vague notion of advancement and of the triumph of the will. Basically, social Darwinism. Yet hardly anyone asks what we are progressing to, when human life holds less and less value. In fact, it seems to be the case that people know things are worse than they have ever been, yet they still believe we are on the road to Utopia.

Building on this, since human beings are just accidents, and nature is not a thing created for us to admire or tend, scientists have become more and more brazen in manipulating it; "improving" it with such genius ideas as splicing spider DNA into the corn supply. And then you have eugenicist elites, who have been "improving" their family lines by breeding selectively. But third and worst is how the Government has targeted the poor and marginalized with magnanimous "improvement agencies" like Planned Parenthood (located conveniently right next to your inner city).

The tide of Darwinism just builds and builds, collecting strength among inconceivable agencies like the aforementioned Planned Parenthood, which obtained its ideology from the grotesque Margaret Sanger. In the hands of such a powerful political will, Darwin, mixed with a dash of Nietzsche, is turned into an assassin's arrow. Once the absence of meaning has been joined to the will to power, the result is selective assassination, carried out with cold calculation, and with a winning smile.

Truth is such a delicate thing, isn't it? Especially in the hands of craven pseudo-scientists, or dangerous pseudo-intellectuals like Adolf Hitler, who couldn't tell the difference between sketches and art. Neither could he apprehend that egregious Darwinian spin-off concepts like "the evolution of the races", should perhaps not be used to annihilate entire peoples. But in the void left within such a mind as his, bereft of healthy human absolutes, a Hitler will still search for them in some dark corner.

And speaking of dark corners, isn't it bizarre, in our post-Enlightenment age, where we have been taught that "man is the measure of all things", that what has resulted from this is a precipitous fall in man's value? Ironically enough, when you make man the only measure, eliminating Transcendence, you end up throwing said progress out the window, as I've argued here and here. [On Man As A Transcendant Being and On The Spirit Of Rights And Remaking The World]

Well, if man is the measure, and he is just an accident, then what does it really matter if he lives or dies? What does he really have to live for? Ah, you see, that's how the mind works. A man must live for something, must believe in something, must look up to something.

And now more questions keep popping up. Given evolution as a fact, what's to stop one group from saying another is not "fully human", is not "human yet", or is no longer "useful"? And why shouldn't they reason thus, if human beings are merely evolving animals?

This grey area is a vast minefield. And you can see the effects of it in the art we create; as we exalt the ugly, the more we internalize the meaningless.

To state the crux again, the theory of evolution strikes directly at the very core of the human mind. And man, who must believe to live, has stopped believing, which has led to everything from abortion to Marxist mass murder.

At heart, man wants to Transcend, have faith, and believe in absolutes; but his own systems wage war against him - nonsensically - crippling his reason, and crushing him by strength of number.

And since I hold that man's ultimate end is to know Perfection, I often wonder what force could be mobilizing mankind to create and sustain such worthless deadly doctrines as Darwinism, without a shred of evidence for them, except that they "must be". Well, why must they be? Because God cannot?

As such, evolution acts as the assassin's arrow; aiming indirectly at the Source of life, by striking at Its image and likeness.

But before it can strike the body, it first must strike the mind.

Is "Hamlet" A Coded Rebuke Of The Evil Tudor Dynasty?

I am thy father's spirit, doom'd for a certain term to walk the night…

Shakespeare's Hamlet has been looked at from myriad angles, from the psychological to the philosophical.

But for me, the key to the drama is this oft overlooked fact: that what drives the plot is that Hamlet's father is a spirit come back from purgatory (the place of purification before entering heaven).

This is really quite remarkable, given that the play was put on in Elizabethan England, a place where the Government had recently repudiated the Catholic Church (and whose censors were very strict regarding dramatic content). Hamlet's father's ghost would have been recognizable to anyone as belonging to the old/outlawed order of ideas; and, if you ask me, Shakespeare brought him back from the dead, in order to resurrect what the murdered King symbolically represents: the ancient Faith, and all the theology that was buried by Henry VIII.

I can only imagine the subdued ooh's and ah's, as the groundlings beheld this monarchic outlaw, passing portentous judgment on the unfaithful Queen, and her incestuous new marriage. A person could be forgiven, if the confluence of ideas caused him to believe that Hamlet was a coded rebuke of the Tudor Kings; who were, themselves, unfaithful to their Divine Spouse.

How did this play ever make it onto the stage, you might ask?! Well, remember, this is "Denmark", not England. And though I believe such heady subtext does exist within the play, it easily becomes lost due to the fiery theatrics and clever wordplay.

It can't be overstated that Hamlet's father's ghost, who is "doom'd for a certain term" to suffer "tormenting flames", is what sets the entire plot in motion. This purgatorial theodrama, unabashedly inserted into the public arena, reflects directly on the Dynasty that banned it; killed it, essentially; just like the play's new King, Claudius, killed Hamlet's father. The death of the "Catholic King" is the central element of the play, and the conviction of the killer, the resolution. Along the way, the incestuous marriage of the "painted Queen", with her dead husband's inferior brother, is examined; and the whole affair ends in bloodshed (A Tudor specialty).

Speaking of bloodshed, the State was actively persecuting Catholics at that time, even repossessing land owned by the Roman Church. This backdrop provides extra drama to the play, as does the odd history of Henry VIII's choice to divorce his legal wife, and start a new religion out of whole cloth. There were beheadings of Catholics, the pursuit and murder of Lords who wouldn't convert; and, of course, the executions of several of Henry's wives. And then there was "Gloriana"! who finished the job her father started.

Given all this, it seems Shakespeare found a clever way to dramatize the perfidy of Tudor England. Still, quite magnanimously, he makes Hamlet's best friend a Protestant; the venerable Horatio; who has just arrived back in Denmark.

Horatio is a student at Wittenberg, the college where Martin Luther taught! Martin Luther, of course, precipitated the fracture of the Church by posting his 99 Theses on the door of a cathedral. The fact that Horatio attends the school where Luther is teaching is highly significant. Horatio cannot believe in a ghost come back from purgatory, because that is not Protestant dogma. This leads to the famous line, spoken by Hamlet, "There is more in heaven and earth… than is dreamed of in your philosophy." In my opinion, this is directed right at the English monarchy. But in any case, the clash of ideas, and the conflict between Catholicism and Protestantism, goes right to the heart of the play.

Despite the large gap in their theologies, Hamlet and Horatio are wonderfully close friends. Their bond strengthens the connection between Catholic and non-Catholic worlds. Clearly, the unity of Christendom is paramount in the mind of the author.

All importantly, Hamlet's devotion to his father, the "Catholic ghost", is the pivot-point of the entire story. And if "Hamlet" is a critique of Tudor England (and I think this is the case, "Catholic ghost", or no), then it could be argued that the new King, Claudius, is a stand in for Henry VIII; and that Shakespeare has him symbolically murdering the old Faith, in the person of his poisoned brother. Or he could represent the new faith; which, like himself, is an inferior copy of what came before. In a similar way, the Danish Queen can represent either Elizabeth I, or the English Government. But it's clear from context that Shakespeare considers the Queen to be sympathetically ignorant, and the King the true villain.

Further connecting Elsinore and England is the connection between the character Polonius, and the real life Tudor Lord, Robert Cecil. Scholars generally agree Shakespeare was lampooning Cecil in the person of Polonius. Both characters were basically State Secretaries, and in charge of developing young Lords, as well. This historical link grounds Hamlet in a direct way to a member of the Tudor court; which connects the Danish castle right to the throne room of Elizabeth.

For those who support the Oxfordian thesis, which asserts Shakespeare was the 17th earl of Oxford, Edward de Vere, an interesting avenue opens up, here. De Vere grew up in Robert Cecil's household, and actually married his daughter, Anne Cecil. The brilliant de Vere, court playwright to Elizabeth, had a tumultuous relationship with his pompous stepfather, and butted heads with him, often.

Interestingly enough, de Vere's unfairness and jealousy ended up leading to Anne's death. It appears he never got over his guilt. Now, if it is true that de Vere was Shakespeare, then the repeated Shakespearean theme of the tragic heroine, ill-used by a wanton man, becomes all the more understandable. And biographical.

The connection to Anne Cecil, and the tragic heroines, leads right to Ophelia, daughter of Polonius. Really, it's a perfect fit. If the aforementioned drama, which happened in the private life of de Vere, is also the drama of Shakespeare's private life, then Hamlet reflects a deeply autobiographical picture of the playwright - more so than could be imagined previously. You may balk at the notion that Shakespeare was not the man from Stratford; but is it really more comforting to think of him as the man who left his wife nothing more than his "second best bed"? and didn't own any books?

The more Hamlet is grounded in reality, and linked to real individuals, the more its themes reflect the state of England at the time the play was written. If Shakespeare was really an Earl, it would make such perfect sense! Tell me, how could he lampoon famous public figures and get away with it, if he himself was not powerful? After all, Robert Cecil was not the only public figure he went after; nor did he restrain himself from dedicating scintillating material to other Lords (like the Sonnets).

As such, the actor, Shaksper (who appears not to have been able to write his name the same way more than one time), would have made a convenient cover for the English Lord. For whatever reason, it was considered unseemly for a royal to publish poetry and plays, especially on such topics as Sir Thomas More, the Catholic saint martyred by Henry VIII. (Recent scholarship favors the idea that Shakespeare contributed three pages to the play written about him.)

Beyond the fact that Hamlet's plot revolves around a "Catholic ghost" returning to visit judgment on his unfaithful state, there are two symbols yet to explore. The Queen and new King die by drinking from a chalice, in which a poisoned pearl is placed. The chalice may well represent the ritual chalice of the Mass, and the pearl may be a reference to the Pearl of Great Price. The parable of the pearl teaches one ought to sell everything one owns, in order to purchase the only thing with true value, which is God (the Tudor's did the exact opposite, it seems).

Shakespeare may be suggesting, that by destroying the Catholic Church in England, the Tudors had turned the Pearl of Great Price into a poisoned pearl, and the ritual chalice into the perfect place to put it.

Thus, the Queen and King die symbolic deaths, connected to betraying the Faith. "Denmark's" royals are wiped out, and a neighboring state with an ancient claim sweeps in to restore order.

Whatever Shakespeare's personal beliefs were, it seems clear to me that he was very concerned with the dynamics between the divided branches of the Church. These dynamics are what animate Hamlet, and truly bring it's spirit to life. The playwright seems to be using taboo topics against the state, in daringly provocative ways, almost as if he wished to yell fire in a crowded theater. One can only imagine what Elizabeth must have been thinking, as she sat and watched her performance of Hamlet, as the "Catholic King's" murder is re-staged within the drama, as if it were happening before her, as it happened to the new King within the play.

What I wouldn't give to have
seen *Elizabeth's* "conscience caught", that day! This gives "the play's the thing" an entirely new meaning.

That play within a play within reality must have hit her like a ton of bricks. Now, if only we could do the same thing with Hillary Clinton...

On the New Toxic Substances Control Act

The inmates are running the asylum. And by inmates, I mean the freewheeling Chemical Corporations and the Government Agencies that "regulate" them.

Granted, this was not the idea the Washington Post intended to convey as it described the new Bipartisan chemical protection Bill, which is nearing Congressional approval. No, the Post presented its story with the sort of oblivious obscurantism that only a Western paper could affect, doing its best to mix up key information to avoid enlightening the reader. After all, if the reader became enlightened, he might find himself extremely upset due to the total negligence of his Government, supposed Watch Dog publications, and trusted corporations. As such, the Post's article is a bit of a puzzle. I put the pieces together, and this is what I came up with.

The previous "Toxic Substances Control Act", signed into law by President Ford forty years ago, was a complete failure, doing nothing to regulate toxicity. (You may balk at this, but I will show you it's true.) The new "Toxic Act" will "streamline" regulations by federalizing the entire process, thereby further removing power from the States to combat chemical companies. No wonder said companies are lobbying for the Bill!

Now you know you're in trouble when your toxic chemical regulations Bill is sponsored by the very companies that create the toxins. Enter the *American Chemistry Council*, an enormous conglomerate representing various gigantic chemical companies. With their full weight behind the "Toxic Act", the genial support of a Bipartisan Legislature, and the EPA offering "technical assistance", what could go wrong? After all, just because these people acted treacherously before, that doesn't mean they can't be trusted again, does it? Does it, Washington Post? New York Times? CNN? Wall Street Journal?

I've been wracking my brain trying to come up with comments sarcastic enough to do this situation justice. After all, an exhaustive account of the hazardous chemicals foisted upon the American public and presented as being safe, would take an ice age to list properly. Perhaps the EPA felt a similar ennui in the face of so much toxicity, because guess what? According to the Post, "Most consumers assume… chemicals have been tested for safety, when the reality is only a tiny fraction of them have." And "current law lets chemicals go to market after three months even without a thorough federal review."

The reality is no one is looking out for us, and the EPA should not be trusted to solve the problems it helped create.

Moving on, disappointingly, even the environmental groups copped out and got on board with the "Toxic Act". And what are they getting in return? A "Prioritize[d]… review of chemicals stored near drinking water", and an increase in the ability of States to "restrict chemicals" after they have been sold for three and a half years, without a satisfactory federal review. But no promises of change regarding negligence.

Unbelievable.

This begs the question: who is it that will "prioritize" the "review" of the water supply, the EPA? What a joke.

Since past is prologue, here's a little more on the history of the EPA. In the last forty years, eight-thousand chemicals have crossed the desk of this "Protection Agency"; two-hundred have been examined in some degree; five have been regulated. (All this according to the Post.) Let's add it all up. The chemical companies create something in the lab, that something might very well be toxic, the EPA looks the other way, the things gets bought by us and may well lead to pollution, sickness and death. This has been the case for forty years, which establishes a criminal pattern. But instead of a Justice Department indictment, the polluters get a second crack at perfecting their situation?!

So yes, the inmates are running the asylum. And they really must be crazy to run the risk of poisoning so many living beings with so many toxins. Thinking about the extent of the vast damage pollution-toxicity has caused truly boggles the mind. First of all there is the human toll. But then there is the fish, birds and animals, oceans lakes and rivers, the sky, the clouds, the soil and seeds. Anyone with eyes to see can tell these things are dying.

Sometimes I wonder that the world outside doesn't seem to penetrate into the skyscrapers and the halls of Congress.

One can only hope something will wake these mad people up. It must be that power and money on that scale are of themselves toxic, in order to derange otherwise intelligent people so thoroughly.

On Diet Soda, Weight Gain and Aspartame

I don't know about you, but when I do a search on a word like Aspartame, I find the best results always come up first. That's because Google is a disinterested third party, with nothing but your best interests at heart. And when you read things like *Aspartame's safe and healthy,* and *try new organic vegan Aspartame*, then you can rest easy, knowing Google's on the ball, and only the best studies are on the table.

And then there's your friendly neighborhood diet soda. If you were to Google diet soda and weight gain, you might just stop at the top article, so authoritative are the authorities in dismissing the unscrupulous rumor mills that purport to link the two. Did you hear, *all* those disreputable sites cited one study featuring two disgruntled rats? Yes. Every. Single. One.

And that's how the industry keeps people away from relevant information. If only it were the only way!

The truth is that all research into diet soda and weight gain doesn't lead back to one study and a pair of rats. I know this because I kept scrolling and checked out different studies. More convincing research reveals that many times people use diet soda to offset other foods. (Not that you can offset the junk these "dieters" are consuming.) The poor soda drinker, already poisoned by false notions of what constitutes a well-balanced diet, ends up eating junk thinking he's earned it by drinking a healthy beverage. And *that's* how the weight is gained.

Other factors are harder to quantify. Many report strange cravings after drinking the drinks, or the need to eat something sweet to nullify the awful taste left behind by Aspartame, etc. This too can lead to gains.

I can sympathize with people who drink diet soda because of advertising propaganda. What I find hard to understand is how someone can get used to drinking something that tastes so horrible?!

And even though Aspartame's link to cancer is fairly well established (unless you read Google's top site recommendations), rational people who can balance a check book and otherwise perform complicated tasks, simply can't accept that a deadly poison is being sold to them (so briskly) over their friend the Television.

This friend of ours is the prime culprit in the selling of "foods of progress". Ever since its appearance and the advent of TV dinner life, we've been taken down the primrose path regarding ersatz food products: buying into the notion that sugar, butter, cheese and water ought to be improved by us.

But the body was not designed to handle ersatz substances. Our organs, proteins and enzymes were made to assimilate sugar, not Aspartame. So the issue really isn't *can I lose a few pounds by drinking diet soda*. It's *will this product end up eventually killing me?* Or perhaps there will only be neurotoxic effects. That sounds better, doesn't it? And then there are the studies: brain tumors have been found in monkeys that ate it; meanwhile mice developed holes in their brains.

Enter Donald Rumsfeld. As Chairman of Searle, the company that owned Aspartame's patent, he vowed to bombard the skittish FDA (at that time opposed to Aspartame due to its deadly reputation), until he got his pet poison into the food supply. And he succeeded, only later becoming Secretary of Defense. I don't know about you, but the entire situation makes my skin crawl.

There's a certain network of vultures that work in tandem to generate profits, no matter what the cost. They understand the power of images and the drives that motivate people. They know how the body works, but realize there's less money to be made making real food. Slimeballs in advertising display gorgeous models sipping health-poison at the gym, to boost soda sales. Soda giants sell drinks that should be marked with skulls and bones. And who could forget the FDA, which proves to be both polyamorous and impotent at the same time. (That's a real feat, people.)

Oscar Wilde famously said,

"True friends stab you in the front."

The truth about diet drinks, modern foods and the enormous apparatus that sells them, is a hard slap in the face. But once the pain fades and the worthless reasons for drinking diet soda dissipate, sanity can set in.

The truth about public diet is largely the opposite of what we've been told by the so-called authorities. Opposing them is an admirable network of like-minded people, striving against Scylla and Charybdis. The question of food and drink is a human rights issue. And the saying you are what eat has never been truer than it is today.

The Deafening Silence Surrounding Fish Kills

23 million Salmon died this year in Chile due to Algae blooms.[1]

4.5 Million fish of all stripes died in a river in Mexico, and nobody knows why.[2]

220,000 pounds of fish died recently in China. 220,000 pounds. Let *that* sink in.[3]

And here in NC, there is an enormous problem at the Neuse River. According to local sources, as many as One Billion fish have died in the "Noose". That may seem outrageous, but 6.5. million fish washed ashore this year in a single day.[4]

Mass fish deaths are being reported all over the world. Really, there are too many accounts to mention.[5] But fish are not the only

[1] Chow, Lorraine. "23 Million Salmon Dead Due To Toxic Algae Bloom In Chile." Eco Watch. March 10, 2016. http://www.ecowatch.com/23-million-salmon-dead-due-to-toxic-algal-bloom-in-chile-1882188276.html

[2] Hootsen, Jan-Albert; Tucker, Duncan. "Millions Of Dead Fish Mysteriously Surface In Lake In Mexico." Vocativ. September 8, 2014. http://www.vocativ.com/world/mexico-world/fish-kill-environment/

[3] Hootsen, Jan-Albert; Tucker, Duncan. "Millions Of Dead Fish Mysteriously Surface In Lake In Mexico." Vocativ. September 8, 2014. http://www.vocativ.com/world/mexico-world/fish-kill-environment/

[4] "Neuse River Fish Kills September 24 Through October 27, 2012." North Carolina Riverkeepers And Waterkeeper Alliance. Riverlaw.us. http://www.riverlaw.us/fishkills.html

[5] Snyder, Michael. "Mass Fish Deaths: Millions Have Been Found Dead All Over The World In The Past Month." End Of The American Dream. May 20, 2014. http://endoftheamericandream.com/archives/mass-fish-deaths-millions-have-been-found-dead-all-over-the-world-in-the-past-

animals dying. More than a million birds and mammals die yearly from eating plastic. And noise pollution in the oceans is causing whales and dolphins to essentially go crazy, beaching themselves to get away from our machines.[6]

Here in America, where fish kills seem to happen in the greatest numbers, the noise level surrounding bombastic campaigns rattles every ear drum; imprecations leveled at Syria saturate the air-waves; and the debate over bathrooms echoes ad nauseam. Meanwhile, a deafening silence surrounds the mass death of aquatic life.

Granted, there is *some* internet coverage provided by main stream news sources. But that's about as far as it goes.

If Television covers the phenomena, it will be local coverage, with citizens expressing outrage, and a local anchor nodding with studied compassion. As everyone knows, a story has to make the leap to national Television to be taken seriously by the masses. Until it appears digitally, it's like it hasn't happened..

The majority of fish kill coverage comes from alternative media sources. But you already knew that! That the main stream would neglect to cover fish kills is all the more striking, considering a chief element of the food supply is at risk. Not to mention the drinking water. But as far as water is concerned, we've been putting up with aquatic pollution for decades. It was only a matter of time before the life went out of the water. What did we think was going to happen, that fairies were going to rescue us? The media's momentary outrage notwithstanding, why haven't we as human beings demanded change? Why do we put up with so much garbage?

---

month
[6] Geer, Abigail. "5 Ways Water Pollution Is Killing Animals." Care2.com. April 3, 2014. http://www.care2.com/causes/5-ways-water-pollution-is-killing-animals.html

4.5 Million #fish of all stripes died in a river in Mexico, and nobody knows why.

Speculation runs rampant as to the cause of the kills. That is, speculation runs rampant among the small number of informed individuals, who discuss it in internet articles, conversations at cafes, or bicker about it in the comments sections of articles (you know who you are, comment assassins).

In the oceans, the top candidates for fatalities are radiation from Fukushima, rubbish and runoff (did you hear, the ocean is now an enormous trash compactor?). In lakes and rivers, the answer (more than likely) is also pollution.

I suppose if media started covering fish kills, since we live in an egalitarian society, they'd also have to cover the poison giant that handles a large portion of the food supply; the animals (destined for food consumption) that live in squalor, pumped up with antibiotics; the vegetables reared in spray; *and then on top of that*, report what's being done to the fish. But with Trump and Cruz going at it like true champions, what's a few hundred million fish in the grand scheme of things?

As any fisherman will tell you, it's getting harder and harder to catch fish these days. Eventually we might just outfish the planet. Then it would be the land animals that disappear. And what then? Federal Reserve Notes dipped in hot sauce?

The extent to which we've poisoned the world really is astonishing. But my guess is you won't hear about it in the news till the last fish is dead. Then CNN will run endless retrospectives on the fish kill phenomena, as if they didn't know it was happening the whole time.

In my last satire I joked about Millennials thinking they could reTweet the fish population. But unlike paper money, digitized Hollywood movies, meat glue and pink slime, real biological life cannot be created ex nihilo by human beings.[7]

So far this article has focused on the utility of aquatic animals. But they are not just food. They're the life of the oceans and fresh water courses. Can you imagine the world without them? The sky without birds? The fields without animals? This could be the future, if we're not careful. As in *The Simpons,* we can create holograms of the last tree, the last whale, and the last human being, or we can wise up and start to value life more than money.

Until that time, please don't tell me the world is progressing, or you might just find yourself sleeping with the fishes.

---

[7] Veritas, Chris. "Six Billion Fish Die In One Day, News Eclipsed By Kardashian Selfie." Some Cry Wolf. April 28, 2016.
http://somecrywolf.blogspot.com/2016/04/six-billion-fish-die-in-one-day-news.html

On Wisdom, The Health Of The World

Her spirit is intelligent,
holy, wholly unique, cogent;
in loving, unassailable,
in blessing, irresistible.

Ours is an age of folly, masquerading as an enlightened epoch.

This is indeed an irony, for we are constantly told humanity is progressing and life is getting better. What standard are they using to measure this, for goodness' sake?! (Oh, yes, it's the *double standard*. Makes sense now.)

It's true that advancements in technology have brought about progress in the world of machines. That is great if you're a machine. If not, even though a world of possibility has opened up, this cannot compensate for the emerging control grid and the war machine's outlandish capacities.

Have we forgotten that with human beings, paradoxes and dark-side realities always accompany the advances we make? That if we aren't careful, greed will ruin the good intentions of the majority? This is Wisdom, to know oneself. To know humanity, its history, potential, and tendencies. Such knowledge leads to health: the health of bodies, minds, and souls, if applied with understanding. But if it isn't, sickness results.

Have we ever been sicker? We produce foods filled with foolish ingredients, which cause disease, yet few are concerned. The remedies are harsh and damaging, yet few complain. Our minds are disturbed by myriad neuroses, and the institutions (also sick) that "treat" us prescribe dangerous cures. But people accept this as the status quo. And our souls, who even thinks about his soul today? To care about one's soul is wise.

Wisdom is love. Whereas the foolish philosophy of the modern world is codified selfishness. This selfishness leads to incredible absurdities, like considering corporations to be people that need protection, while the homeless are scattered and (in some places) even criminalized.

Why is love wise? It looks after human beings. It scatters charity, not humanity; seeks the benefit of the many; cherishes life, increases health, and builds civilization through diplomacy and sacrifice.

Wisdom is wise use of knowledge.

As far as knowledge goes, the astute have caught on that the root of our modern problems began in the Renaissance and Enlightenment. Since man was made "the measure of all things", and it was declared that "institutions can change human nature", because all men are "blank slates", more men have been killed and enslaved than at any other time in recorded history. Making mankind-alone our ideal does not seem to be wise, because man is a weak creature, who must transcend himself to flourish.

Wisdom means looking up and admiring Eternal Beauty. This is a means of transcendence and leads to life. Man admiring himself becomes myopic, and turns other men into objects of conquest. We're seeing the fullness of this play out today, as all over the world, people are divided over ideology, ethnicity, and borders; one group stands on the left, another on the right, each furiously shaking its fists at the other. Hardly a region of the earth is not effected. It's like we've all gone mad by drinking wolfbane.

The wise understand our problems begin from within, but are accentuated by bad teaching. Humanities' flaws recycle themselves and are accentuated when ignored, as Tabula Rasa does. On the other hand, we have the ability to overcome human nature (don't you think?), but it must be acknowledged that we have one in the first place! Otherwise, we may increasingly flounder about, rearranging the deck chairs on the Titanic, till the cold water hits.

To acknowledge the past is Wisdom. To proceed with deliberation is intelligent. To honor the health of the body, the mind, and the spirit, is indispensable. All the while shoring up weaknesses in human beings and the systems we create. None of this is being done today. Instead, institutions trample on the very beings they're designed to serve, lessons from the past are forgotten, and all our acquired Wisdom is scorned by those who consider themselves the gatekeepers of knowledge and societal welfare.

This is the height of folly.

The modern world may be ruled by intelligent idiots, but this doesn't disclude us from personally growing in Wisdom. Ages come and go, but the light of life is carried by the wise, who know how to preserve the integrity of civilization, even through bleak epochs that masquerade as paragons ablaze.

Sleep Hacks That Are Suited To The Modern World

Last Sunday, I was hanging out with Heather Callaghan and Brandon Turbeville, two writers no one who reads this site frequently should be unfamiliar with. We were brainstorming topics for my next article. They suggested I write on sleep. Wouldn't you know it, I assented, and couldn't sleep for the next three days!

It's not that I did anything differently, mind you. But sleep is a fragile thing, and oft eludes, inexplicably.

Backing up a bit, Heather, Brandon and I, first came up with a set of things that don't aid sleep at all (satirists that we are). But not satisfied with what we'd done, we augmented the list with a second set of tips; this time suggesting ways of achieving sleep; and once achieving it, keeping it going throughout the night. I hope you find they work well for you. .

How not to get to sleep

1: Worry about sleep. The sleep process is not simply biological, it's also psychological. If you read my article on Ambien Zombies, you already know women suffer from insomnia in greater numbers than men. On this point, a female friend of mine asserted this is because women are more sensitive than men, and therefore worry more. (Whereas I assumed it was due to something like neurotransmitters.) With this in mind, when it's time for sleep, one must leave thought behind. We'll cover suggestions for doing this, later.

2: Worry about other things. Easier said than done, I know. Anxiety over daily events, and thoughts about tomorrow, come in crowds. To shut out these voices, many turn to sleep aids to find rest. Excuse me, "sleep aids". I put these words in quotes because, as I've discovered, the leading "solutions" from Big Pharma are pathetic products, and dangerous in the main. When approaching sleep, the day you just experienced, and the day to come, must fade into oblivion. I suggest rethinking the nighttime ritual.

3: Take Ambien. Some of you may be saying, "Hey, now! I get great sleep when I take Ambien". Nope. You're not asleep, you're hypnotized. My advice to you is, if you take this product, chain yourself to the bed. Because if it so happens that you suddenly "turn zombie", and, let's say, run someone over without knowing it, the courts have determined it's your own darn fault.[8]

4: Take Halcion. Once again, we're talking hypnosis, not sleep. Plus, Halcion has a reputation for inducing psychotic episodes and suicide. I personally believe when it comes to drifting off, the best way to go about this is to gently induce it, with natural products.[9]

5: Watch the news before bedtime. This can only lead to more worry. In all seriousness, are the networks trying to make Americans insomniacs? Avoid the news, if you want to relax at bedtime.

6: Sleep next to your cell phone or tablet. Certain people swear that doing this disrupts sleep rhythms, due to electric current emanating from these devices. Either way, having them nearby increases the risk of being woken by a call, or reaching down to check something. How about this? Turn them off, leave them in the living room, and go to sleep for goodness' sake.

7: Drink coffee and soda after 4 PM. It's 7:35 PM right now, and I'm drinking a cup of dark roast java. Feel free to mock. But let me pass on this bit of information. Caffeine stays in the blood stream for six hours, so if you're like me, you'll be dealing with its effects well into the night. Food for thought.

---

[8] Drugs.com – Ambien. http://www.drugs.com/ambien.html

[9] Drugs.com – Halcion. http://www.drugs.com/pro/halcion.html

In addition to these detracting factors, I would add that temperature, light, noise, and the comfort of one's bed, make a world of difference when snoozing time rolls around.

Now, on to some tips for sleep achievement.

1: Have a sleep ritual. You can't just bounce from a stressful state to a non-stressed state. Those whose lives are generally relaxing may be able to do this, but for the rest of us, it will take some doing. Which means it's good to create a transition state, a relaxation bubble, to ease mind and body into. I would suggest devoting an hour to this, detaching from TV and mobile devices. Put on some PJ's. Sit in a comfortable chair. Or perhaps…

2: Take a warm bath. *And…*

3: Read a book. *While…*

4: Drinking sleepy time tea.

5: Take 1 mg of Melatonin, dissolving it under the tongue. It's paradoxical, but when it comes to Melatonin, less is more. Also, I've heard nothing but good things about the dissolvable form.

6: Magnesium spray. This one comes from Heather Callaghan, who swears by this method. One caveat. Some may need to dilute it, if they have sensitive skin.

7: Love, forgive, accept, meditate; and if you believe in God, be sure to pray. My belief is a great source of consolation. Think about it. Everything we do depends on faith. Part of the nightly ritual could be dedicated to looking up and admiring the stars, and at least wondering, "how is it that there is something out there, and not nothing at all?"

You'll notice the preceding list is primarily focused on ways of approaching sleep that accentuate relaxation, and chemicals come last. It's this writer's opinion that sleep must be induced gently. Big Pharma takes a sledgehammer to the process, to get dramatic results. If you're a desperate insomniac, I won't begrudge you if you take Ambien. But again, buy yourself a set of shackles, and manacle yourself to the bed. It might just save you serving twenty years to life.

To round out the article, let's take a look at…

A few things that can disrupt your circadian rhythms.

1: Cigarettes. If you're a smoker, don't you find yourself waking up with cravings from time to time?

2: Alcohol. A misconception exists that alcohol assists sleep, but the opposite is true.

3: Light. The eye is made to detect light. Do all you can to create total darkness, to maximize deep sleep.

4: Foods to avoid: chili dogs and MSGs. At least for dinner. MSG-laced foods give me horrific nightmares, and chili dogs are hard to digest, which can cause the same result.

It's no wonder so many people have trouble sleeping. The forty hour work week, the war on terror, and the things we eat, drink, and amuse ourselves with, seem allied against holistic rest. But fortunately, the process can be assisted with a few adjustments. I hope this article is helpful to you. Dors bien!

Seven Health Hacks That Truly Work Wonders

It's a mystery how this writer has never written an article on health before, given that the past thirteen years have been fully dedicated to it! In 2002 I had surgery for a non-metastasizing tumor in the right chest. Although the surgery was a success, it left me with "hospital pneumonia"; eight chest tubes; and a reconstructed chest wall, with the right arm devoid of support-muscles. Oh, did I mention the surgery took seventeen hours?

A year and a half later, the tumor came back; and I received the maximum radiation one can be prescribed, which put me in hospice, twice (this was because the doctors thought the growth would not respond... at all). Fortunately, the mass did end up shrinking; but I was sick for several years, basically subsisting on bread for nourishment.

Slowly I've made gains in strength. And after battling an array of health issues, and researching various cures, I've learned a good deal about what works. Now, I'd like to pass on a few excellent tips to you, which we will call, "My seven health hacks".

1) Turmeric. You can buy it either in powdered form, or in the form of a capsule. Either way, turmeric is powerful at fighting infection, inflammation, and even pain (due to inflammation, of course). From personal experience, I can tell you it is powerful enough to fight off a bone infection. It's also a strong anti-cancer preventative.

As far as using the root powder, it can stain, and the taste is a bit strong. I personally mix it with a shake, and that masks most of the flavor. For those who wish to avoid these things, I would advise going with the capsule. Either way, get the turmeric, and use it everyday.

2) Manuka Honey. Do you have a wound that won't close; an abrasion that resists healing; acid reflux; or a sinus infection? If so, google these problems and "Manuka honey". This beautiful product from New Zealand has incredible curative powers; and I can personally attest that it closes wounds, as it did with the one I had that was due to radiation. It's an amazing product, that can potentially prevent surgeries, and deflect expensive "purple pill" purchases.

3) Tired all the time? Check your thyroid; iron; and vitamin D levels. A drop in any one of these could be what is causing it, and a simple blood test will indicate the results to you. Besides energy gain, people taking thyroid medicine report significant weight loss; iron users report interesting things such as the return of thinning hair; and vitamin D users speak of gains in bone density, and even greater joy! Highly recommended.

4) Turmeric, honey, and black pepper. This mixture is a powerful decongestant. I'm prone to congestion, myself, having had pneumonia after my surgery. Only 24 hours after I first tried this, I started coughing stuff up. An albuterol nubulizer also works, but many will not want to inhale the chemical.

I recommend using a measuring cup to mix it in. Then take 4-5 oz. of honey, 3 tea spoons of turmeric, and a dash of the black pepper, and stir till mixed thoroughly.

5) For the elderly, the slight, and the sick, I recommend making protein shakes. Personally, I mix a vanilla shake in with mint chocolate chip ice cream, and one banana; but others use yogurt, especially those who are watching their sugar. (And as I mentioned previously, a shake is a great way to take your ground turmeric.)

Although most today seem to be trying to lose weight, for the frail, the elderly, and the thin, who are in danger of falling and hurting themselves, a little padding is always helpful. Protein can also give you an energy boost. Worth considering.

6) Garlic. Great for sore throats and colds, and also an anti-inflammatory, garlic is a staple for the do-it-yourself-doctor.

7) Stillness. Rest. Contemplation. Generosity. Gratitude.

What's the point of having a well-tuned body, if your soul is agitated and conflicted? Human beings are more than just bodies, and the interior must be nourished as well.

I learned these hacks over time, but you can employ them instantly. The good news is that certain things that we live with and sometimes have serious operations for, can be healed with quite simple remedies. I also recommend taking a good multi-vitamin, and exercising, too.

I wish you luck, and perfect health!

The Secret Lives Of Ambien Zombies

Have you ever stripped naked on a plane without cognition, cooked a meal in the middle of the night unawares, or woken up in some strange place, not knowing how on earth you got there? If so, you might be an Ambien Zombie.

As far as we know, the term "Ambien Zombie" descends from the flight attendant community. These poor flight attendants follow a simple code; if you spot a problem, it's yours to fix. Which means that if the Zombie streaking past your station urinates in the aisle nearest you, you get the blest job of cleaning it up and restraining him.

Story after story has been related of bad behavior on flights, performed by passengers who have taken Ambien to fight jet lag. While asleep, they become a nightmare for attendants; strange, unreachable, id driven creatures, shuffling down the aisles with blank expressions. That being said, Ambien's intended use is directed more towards insomnia and sleep deprivation. Not that all mind its intended use.

The Ambien Zombie phenomenon occurs only in a minority of cases. But these cases are so striking, damaging, and dangerous, that, many times, the lives of its users are altered and/or ruined forever.

But hey, that's just part of the cost of doing business. So, with that in mind, here are a few slogans I invented to help Sanofi Aventis sell their beloved drug more adequately.

"Ambien; don't mix it with alcohol, for pity's sake!"

"Ambien; see you tomorrow, honey, if you don't kill me in my sleep."

And, "Ambien; at least it's not Halcyon."

Speaking of Halcyon (a former market leader in sleep aids, and accidental psychosis and suicide inducer), can't we do better than this?

After all, the aim is to induce sleep, not create mental patients, right? Right?

By the way, Halcyon is still on the market. Shocking, I know.

But back to Ambien Zombies. Numerically, the majority are women, because women suffer from insomnia in greater numbers than men. Thus, they are more likely to incur the drug's odd side effects, such as "strange behavior" and "abnormal thinking". (Huh. These are acceptable drug reactions?) An added danger to women is the sad likelihood that Ambien will be used to facilitate rape. Not only does said product increase arousal, it also short-circuits memory; which makes it ideal for predators who want to get away scot free. Rohypnol is difficult to come by, but not Ambien, which is only a schedule six drug.

A certain portion of people use Ambien not as a sleep aid, but as a sex stimulant (see Tiger Woods). Some use it to get high, fighting to stay awake in order to ride out on its psychedelic buzz. Many, I imagine, are quite surprised to find their sleep aid makes them trip out, and/or feel like Rick James! (May he rest in peace.)

Those with more normal designs have found themselves unwittingly "sleep driving", "sleep shopping", and "sleep eating". As to the "sleep eaters", they might not end up cooking brains, but they've been known to make such lustrous fare as buttered cigarettes, as one surprised Zombie reported, upon awaking.

In fairness to the FDA, they've responded to all this with typical professionalism; ordering Sanofi to "issue stronger warning labels". Thanks, FDA. You guys are the best.

In light of this development, please allow me to suggest an updated label of my own. "Ambien may cause you to walk off a cliff without knowing it. Thanks, Sanofi."

As an Ambien Zombie, you may one day find yourself waking up in jail, charged with a DWI and/or homicide you don't remember. If this happens, you might attempt the new "Zombie Defense" others have made who've gone before. When this fails, you're welcome to "try" suing Sanofi. (Good luck there.) For those not yet arrested, who still insist on taking Ambien, may I suggest buying a set of shackles and manacling yourself to the bed? This ought to avert any potential episodes. Be sagacious; that's the ruling of the courts. If you don't prevent yourself from turning Zombie, it's your own darn fault, buddy.

Let's be realistic, when it comes to insomnia, it's ridiculous to expect a sleep deprived person to be so sagacious. By the time you get to that point, you're so desperate for sleep, not only are you probably not reading the warning label, you might even be willing to risk anything to get relief. In any case, who would expect a drug sold with such a delightful butterfly to be dangerous? I'm surprised there aren't puppies jumping around on the bed.

As far as the class of Zombies who use Ambien for pleasure, these are playing roulette, and deserve less sympathy. One has to wonder at the person who, over and over, takes this drug and winds up in some strange place. On the other hand, the high from the drug is so attractive, it may just override the conscious mind. (Wow. Yet another example of how this happens.) Speaking of Ambien abusers, some don't even have to take the drug to do so; but I would still classify them as the walking dead.

No matter how dramatic and tragic, the preceding information remains mostly overlooked. Perhaps this is because, if it were to get out, by means of Hollywood, Television, or the Press, a certain drug company might lose its multi-billion dollar cash cow? That leaves little bloggers like me to take up the strain, alone against a deafening silence.

Instead of witnessing to the truth, Hollywood's given us countless tales of fictional zombies, sloughing through the night in search of brains, who disappear mysteriously by day; while in reality, a living class of walking dead also disbrain, only to find themselves in the morning, mysteriously full again.

There are millions of Ambien users, worldwide. I wonder how many of them have similar stories? How many, I wonder, were lured into buying Ambien by that beautiful butterfly, only to find it was glowing because it's radioactive?

Ironically, Ambien is a nightmare.

Paradoxically, it's even worse than Rohypnol.

And sarcastically, I'd like to say to the FDA, "You stay classy, San Diego."

Ah, the FDA. It truly is one killer organization.

Why Are These 25 Carcinogens Still Being Sold?

The FDA is a killer organization.

So superior are they, and so very post-modern, that it seems they've transcended meaning, analysis, and the law of cause and effect. Given their exalted status, should it really surprise that they've not noticed the myriad ways they've advanced the march of carcinogens? After all, it's not like they run studies, check results, or have some sort of mandate to protect, right?

With this in mind, let's examine a few of the carcinogens approved, ignored, and/or excused by the FDA; whose motto really ought to be, "move along, there's nothing to see, here".

1) Baby Powder. The talc in this powder is linked to ovarian cancer. The FDA's response? Too much money at stake to investigate. Very nihilistic, FDA! Nietzsche would approve.[10]

2) Cosmetics. It's a beautiful thing that the cosmetics industry uses industrial factory cleaners to pulchrify womankind, don't you think? No regulation needed here, folks. Even though said chemicals have been found to cause cancer, disrupt hormones, and presage early puberty. I mean, the FDA is really busy. You can't expect them to examine everything, can you?[11]

---

[10] What Is Wrong With Baby Powder?" The Alternative Daily.
http://www.thealternativedaily.com/what-is-wrong-with-baby-powder/

[11] "Clear Science: Environmental Breast Cancer Links." Breast Cancer Fund.
http://www.breastcancerfund.org/clear-science/environmental-breast-cancer-links/cosmetics/

3) Birth control. The estrogen and progesterone within birth control have been found to "lead to cancer". But since there's no "smoking gun", why "rock the boat"? After all, "the show must go on". "It's just business". And an investigation might just "kill profit margins". Priorities, folks. Priorities.[12]

4) Fluoride. Harvard scientists have found that boys in their 6th, 7th, and 8th years, are highly susceptible to osteosarcomas related to fluoride. Add to this the fact that fluoride is a mutagen, which means it alters DNA, and a neurotoxin, and it becomes quite clear the FDA is right to be unconcerned about allowing fluoride in our drinking water. Good job, old sport. Keep earning our trust.[13]

5) Pesticides. Roughly 60% of pesticides lead directly to cancer. But the EPA seems rather bored with this statistic. Now, there has been "some news lately", about a "new standard", that's "less deadly". Whatever. It's the circle of life. We have to put toxins on our crops that will kill us, so that the food we reap can keep us alive till we die. Can't you people understand this?![14]

6) Sugar. A large part of the Standard American Diet (S.A.D.), sugar makes America go! Oh, did I mention sugar exponentially increases the growth of cancer cells? Well, too bad. We have to have it, cells or no. Whether it's in soda, candy, or children's cereal (aka sugar), the FDA is right to sleep on this one. Otherwise, how could people stay awake during the endless forty-hour work week?[15]

---

[12] "Clear Science: Radiation Chemicals and Breast Cancer." Breast Cancer Fund. http://www.breastcancerfund.org/clear-science/radiation-chemicals-and-breast-cancer/oral-contraceptives.html

[13] "Cancer." Fluoride Alert.org http://fluoridealert.org/issues/health/cancer/

[14] "Pesticide-Induced Diseases: Cancer." Beyond Pesticides. http://www.beyondpesticides.org/resources/pesticide-induced-diseases-database/cancer

7) Aspartame. This sweetener/carcinogen was rescued from oblivion by Monsanto, who bought out the agency that was challenging it's production. Listed as "toxic poison" by those in the know, Aspartame causes so many disorders it would take a separate article to cover to them all. Suffice it to say, the FDA and Monsanto are class acts, that obviously care deeply about human life. You stay classy, San Diego.[16]

8) Ersatz Sugar and Diet Cola. Aspartame, Aspartame, Aspartame. People reason taking this toxic carcinogen (which many KNOW is such) makes more sense than consuming real sugar, which might cause them to put on weight. At least I think that's why they do it. After all, who in their right mind would choose Aspartame for its flavor? To summarize, many otherwise bright individuals voluntarily put a foul tasting chemical into their bodies, that might kill them, to (potentially) keep trim. Ironically, Aspartame may just be making Americans a lot fatter.

9) Smoking. Fifteen different types of cancer are caused by cigarettes, which contain six-hundred "ingredients", that when burned, turn into *seven-thousand chemicals, **sixty-nine of which cause cancer**.* Too bad you can't smoke Aspartame, eh, Phillip Morris?[17]

---

[15] Mercola, Joseph. "Sugar Identified As A Top Cause Of The Surge In Cancer." Mercola.com
http://articles.mercola.com/sites/articles/archive/2016/01/20/sugar-top-cause-cancer-surge.aspx

[16] "Aspartame: By Far The Most Dangerous Substance Added To Most Foods Today." Mercola.com.
http://articles.mercola.com/sites/articles/archive/2011/11/06/aspartame-most-dangerous-substance-added-to-food.aspx

[17] "15 Types of Cancer Caused By Smoking." Quitshisha.
http://www.quitshisha.com/blog/cancer/15-types-of-cancer-caused-by-smoking/

10) Cell Phones. The WHO believes cell phones are "possibly carcinogenic", and French researchers have found there is a threefold added risk of brain tumor growth in cell users with 900 plus hours exposure. Swedish researchers have concluded there is a similar risk for those who've used them twenty-five years or more. The main stream governmental and scientific community's response to this? "Yeah, right! Nobody messes with progress." It's business before pleasure, and by pleasure, I mean human life.[18]

11) Soy. Eating soy "may" turn on genes linked to cancer growth. And right now, I "may" be thinking of sarcastic things to say about our regulatory agencies. But I digress.[19]

12) BPA. According to Forbes, BPA is not harmful. (Thanks, guys; clearly there's no conflict of interest.) Now, on to what real scientists are saying. Apparently BPA disrupts genes that defend against cancer. So, okay, maybe it doesn't CAUSE cancer, but it helps the things that cause cancer cause cancer. So please be sure not to touch or eat from plastic containers anymore, or handle glossy receipts. (Oh, wait, that's impossible.) Now, moving on to more things Forbes probably isn't worried about.[20]

---

[18] Coureau, Gaelle; Bouvier, Ghislaine; Lebailly, Pierre; Fabbro-Peray, Pascale; Gruber, Anne; Leffondre, Karen; Guillamo, Jean-Sebastien; Loiseau, Hugues; Mathoulien-Pelissier, Simone; Salamon, Roger; Baldi, Isabella; "Mobile Phone Use And Brain Tumorus In The CERENAT Case Control Study." British Medical Journal. May 9, 2014. http://oem.bmj.com/content/early/2014/05/09/oemed-2013-101754?sid=bb168dfc-bb3d-41c4-bcf9-b5b75d64a8c3

[19] "Eating Soy May Turn On Genes Linked To Cancer Growth." BreastCancer.org. http://www.breastcancer.org/research-news/soy-may-turn-on-genes-linked-to-cancer

[20] "BPA Linked To Breast Cancer Tumor Growth." Science Daily. March 6, 2014. https://www.sciencedaily.com/releases/2014/03/140306163359.htm

13) Acetaminophen. Risk of blood cancer doubles for users of this pain-killer.[21]

14) Statins. Speaking of drugs that effect the blood, several statins have been found to be carcinogenic. Now if that doesn't raise your pressure, nothing will.[22]

15) GMOs. A major study found recently that GMO maize caused cancer in lab rats.[23] Surprisingly, the study was tabled. They say money doesn't grow on trees, but the way Monsanto and the GMO crowd create organic anomalies, I'm starting to wonder. And where was the FDA in all of this? Oh, right! Drinking cocktails with Hillary Clinton at O'Malley's Irish Pub. Clearly there's something wrong with you if you don't favor crossing human genes with corn, or corn with the hepatitis virus. That's just progress.[24] I mean, how could such things go wrong?

---

[21] Jaslow, Ryan. "Acetominophen Linked To Cancer: How Big Is The Threat?" CBS News. May 10, 2011. http://www.cbsnews.com/news/acetaminophen-linked-to-cancer-how-big-is-the-threat/

[22] Ravnskov, Uffe; Rosch, Paul J.; McCully, Kilmer S. "Statins Do Not Protect Against Cancer: Quite The Opposite." Journal of Clinical Oncology. DOI: 10.1200/JCO.2014.58.9564 *Journal of Clinical Oncology* 33, no. 7 (March 2015) 810-811.

PMID: 25605834

[23] Walia, Arjun. "New Study Links GMOs To Cancer, Liver/Kidney Damage & Severe Hormonal Disruption." Collective Evolution. July 15, 2014. http://www.collective-evolution.com/2014/07/15/new-study-links-gmos-to-cancer-liverkidney-damage-severe-hormonal-disruption/

[24] "About GMOs" Non GMO Shopping Guide. http://www.nongmoshoppingguide.com/about-gmos.html

16) Pollution. File this one under "part of the cost of doing business". Seems we can't create profits without creating poison, or create poison without turning it into food.[25]

17) Microwave ovens. Swiss researcher Hans Hertel has concluded that when we eat microwaved food, our cells form emergency anaerobic environments in response, the exact condition which leads to cancer cell growth. But don't worry, the internetz is full of edumacational articles saying the opposite.[26]

18) Lead. Did you know that lead in lipstick may cause cancer? Why is lead in lipstick, anyway? Who was the first person who thought that would be a good idea? Perhaps it's inspired by Hamlet's famous quip, "Here's metal more attractive". Yes, that must be it.[27]

19) Processed meats. These include hot dogs, ham, bacon, sausage, and some deli meats, which have been "treated" to "improve the flavor". Yummy.[28]

[25] Kessler, Rebecca. "Air Pollution's Impact On Cancer Is 'Grossly Underestimated.'" Scientific American. July 1, 2014. https://www.scientificamerican.com/article/air-pollution-s-impact-on-cancer-is-grossly-underestimated/

[26] Fassa, Paul. "Why And How Microwave Cooking Causes Cancer." Natural News. December 8, 2010. http://www.nongmoshoppingguide.com/about-gmos.html

[27] Severns, Maggie. "Which 20 Lipsticks Contain The Most Lead?" Mother Jones. May 6, 2013. http://www.motherjones.com/environment/2013/05/study-lead-metals-lipstick-top-20

[28] Turbeville, Brandon. "WHO Reports That Processed Meats Are Linked To Cancer." Natural Blaze. October 26, 2015. http://www.naturalblaze.com/2015/10/who-reports-that-processed-meats-are-linked-to-cancer.html

20) Gardasil. This vaccine increases the risk of precancerous legions by 44.6%, if the person has already been exposed to HPV 16 or 18, before injection.[29]

21) Research shows **LED bulbs** have tiny cracks in them that release UV rays, which burn skin cells, causing melanoma. (Too bad you can't find the old bulbs anymore.)[30]

22) High fructose corn syrup. How many hundreds of products is this little monster hiding in? It's ubiquity doesn't erase the fact that it's known to cause pancreatic cancer.[31]

23) McDonald's McRib Sandwich. First of all, the entire fast food industry is a disgrace. It puts things in food that just boggle the mind (such as azodicarbonamide, an ingredient Subway once put in their breads. By the way, it's also found in yoga mats.) But the disgusting McRib takes the cake.[32] Chemicals used in soil fertilizer are found in it,

[29] "Does Gardasil Actually Increase Your Risk Of Cervical Cancer?" Mercola.com. July 20, 2010. http://articles.mercola.com/sites/articles/archive/2010/07/20/does-gardasil-actually-increase-your-risk-of-cervical-cancer.aspx

[30] Cohen, Hiyaguha. "Spiral Compact Fluorescents Cause Skin Cancer" or "Do Your Light Bulbs Cause Cancer?" Baseline of Health Foundation. JonBarron.org. February 12, 2015. https://jonbarron.org/cancer-alternative-cancer-therapies/do-your-lightbulbs-cause-cancer#.VtRjgf32blU

[31] Suhaila, Lena. "High Fructose Corn Syrup And Pancreatic Cancer." Natural Medicine Journal. October 2012 Vol. 4. Issue 10. http://www.naturalmedicinejournal.com/journal/2012-10/high-fructose-corn-syrup-and-pancreatic-cancer

[32] Roberts, Jeff. "The 70 Ingredient Cancer Promoting McRib Sandwich: It's Not Real Food." Collective Evolution. November 25, 2013. http://www.collective-evolution.com/2013/11/25/the-70-ingredient-cancer-promoting-mcrib-sandwich-its-not-real-food/

as well as the aforementioned Subway chemical. Plus the pickles are carcinogenic. And the FDA just stands there, hands in its pockets, with a stupid expression, looking like Napoleon Dynamite. Can't you just hear them saying, "Tina you fat lard, come get dinner. Tina! Eat the FOOD!"?

24) Monsanto. Due to this wonderful organization's role in saving Aspartame from destruction, mass-producing GMO's, and filling the world with deadly toxins, I feel Monsanto deserves a special place on this list of carcinogens. Bravo. And props to the FDA for defending us from this monster. You guys are the best.[33]

25) The Standard American Diet (S.A.D.). Let's add things up from the list.[34] Processed meats? Check. Total sugar overload? Check. Aspartame? Check. GMO's, fake cheese, fake juice and brominated bread? Check, check, check, check. Put it in the microwave, and double down on the fun. Or you could just cook a frozen dinner. Everything is encouraged by our friends at the FDA, except cooking organic food, in a natural oven, with real butter and raw milk. In fact, if you produce raw milk, you might just get raided by the FBI.[35]

Why in the world are these twenty-five carcinogens still being sold? And why is proffering poison so fashionable, while pure products

[33] Hanzai E. "The Complete History Of Monsanto, The World's Most Evil Corporation." Waking Times. June 20, 2014.
http://www.wakingtimes.com/2014/06/20/complete-history-monsanto-worlds-evil-corporation/

[34] Danovick, Tove. "The Sad 'Standard American Diet' Is Taking Over The World." Take Part. September 14, 2015.
http://www.takepart.com/article/2015/09/14/global-dietary-illness/

[35] Levaux, Ari. "The Latest Raw Milk Raid: An Attack On Food Freedom?" The Atlantic. August 15, 2011.
https://www.theatlantic.com/health/archive/2011/08/the-latest-raw-milk-raid-an-attack-on-food-freedom/243635/

are priced out of reach? Our world is now suffused with corporately created carcinogens, which build up the bodies of abstract entities, but give living beings the shaft. And all Washington seems concerned with is running Trump vs. Hillary, and bombing the tar out of Syria. Meanwhile, the SAD American diet clearly leads to cancer, and the health machine's one response is to use toxic poison to "help solve the problem".

All sarcasm aside, the FDA, EPA, and the myriad agencies responsible for monitoring food, health, and beauty, are doing such a terrible job, I think it not outlandish to question whether the whole system isn't corrupt, and designed for a tragic end?

Cosmetics, sugar, technology, and fast food: these attractive items are like the glistening fibers of a spider's web. "How could this lovely thing be dangerous", thinks the fly. Little does he know, his appetite for attractive objects is well known to the spider.

The food we're eating is eating us. Our medicine bites, and its oversight sucks. Meanwhile, where has the spider gone? He's hiding behind the Board, looking respectably bespectacled. The last people you would expect to be monsters seem to be the first to profit from human misery. Let's face it, either they really are monsters, or they're so incompetent, they ought to be placed on a short bus. You tell me which alternative makes more sense?

The good news is that, even though the FDA is just awful, we can make lists like this of products to avoid. We don't have to eat ourselves to death by imbibing the likes of Aspartame. And perhaps, with enough awareness, we can put these companies out of business. Viva la revolucion!

Haiku

Pink chemtrail clouds skate

the barium sky; checkmate

for the human race.

On The Spirit of Rights, and Remaking The World

In this day and age, where confusion is rampant, and the inversion of American Principles a thoroughgoing affair, I think it crucial to renew knowledge of the origin of our Rights and Freedoms, that we may the better defend them from their most subtle enemies.

It's an open secret that the Declaration declares the Rights of Americans to be the gift of God, not the gift of Government; which turns said gift into grift. As such, they are not magnanimous largesse, similar to a welfare check or entitlement; but something "inalienable"; which, essentially, means Government derives its power from free persons who "consent" to be governed, and not the other way 'round.

You wouldn't think this is the case, the way the President behaves, and the Courts legislate; as they bypass the people, to push controversial or unpassable policy. (Hey, what ever happened to Sic Semper Tyrannis?)

If the Obama Administration had its way, the revolution in human values would be over.

Extremely telling was the President's speech, on the day when he declared the Beatitudes to be dangerous to Liberty. Either he doesn't understand that this is where the idea of individual Liberty came from; or he does, and he was mounting an indirect assault at it. And frankly, I can't say which is worse.

Let's backtrack a moment. Before the Beatitudes, before Christ, there was the pagan world, which had Rome as its shining pinnacle. Though containing laws and a complex legal code, Rome was extremely venal; and the rich and powerful were favored, while the poor and unconnected were considered expendable. (Sound familiar?) In short, the

State was the true living being, and "goddess Rome", and "divine Caesar", alone, had transcendent importance.[36]

What was the meaning of one human life? A man lived and died, and nothing remained of him. At best, he might be remembered as a hero, and thus obtain some measure of immortality. *Perhaps* for the powerful, the case could be different; if the inscrutable gods were impressed with their prowess. But for ordinary men, there was no eternal life; and thus, no fraternal Rights.

But everything changed after Christ.

Although He was not actively teaching political theory, His ideas still revolutionized the way human beings saw Themselves and their States.

The foundation of this revolution is the idea that all human beings have Spirits, which make them eternal; and, therefore, invaluable. Governments will pass away; stars will pass away; the universe will cease to be; but even the least among humanity will outlive the universe, the stars, and the might of "divine Caesar".

The true spirit of the revolution in Rights is the revelation that Spirit alone gives value to life. (Not that the animals are valueless; in fact, the more spiritual a person is, the more they will tend to care for lesser beings.)

Now, the values of the Spirit are the values of the "peacemaker"; the "meek"; and the "poor in spirit"; that is, those who are not unnaturally attached to riches and power. Not that riches and power are always evils, but they do tend to become inimical to individuals; especially as States advance and become ossified. You will, of course, recognize the Beatitudes, here; but perhaps you didn't realize how

---

[36] Veritas, Chris. "On Man As A Transcendent Being." Natural Blaze. January 20, 2016. http://www.naturalblaze.com/2016/01/on-man-as-a-transcendent-being.html

dangerous they are to the Barack Obamas of the world, or how essential to modern Democracies?

Unlike the way the ancients practiced Democracy (which, in truth, was very little different from a suffragettic Oligarchy), we practice it as an inherently free; voluntarily peaceful; valued citizenry; mostly composed of – get this – ordinary workers! (that is, the "meek"). Truly, the Founders got it right when they linked human Rights to God, because only a God could guarantee the cause of the powerless in this cruel world.

Super Corporatization, Federalization, and all the enormous "isms" of modernity, are like armed men hired out against the individual; and the "subtle" societal campaigns against religion (affecting superiority in the name of Rights), are like a steep road leading us right back to Rome.

To avoid this potentiality, the human Spirit must be held eternal and priceless; this alone places the State beneath our feat.

Otherwise, peoples tend to end up subject to "geniuses" like Marx and Lenin; two materialists who thought their type of State to be the "final revolution" in the history of humanity. (Of course, their "brilliant insights" led to the deaths of nearly 100 million people.) Not to reduce all opposition to a straw man, but it seems the contact of modern, spiritually enlightened Democracies, with atheistic counter-movements, has produced nothing but slaughters.

(Sorry, Karly; the revolution is not of this world.)

Human beings are always trying to create utopias. Regardless of this, I imagine there will continue to be tension between the poor and the rich; Peoples and States; and Spirit and material. This dynamic tension has the power to produce wonders for the world; or make miserable environments, like the Gulag Archipelago.

You see, in the midst of all this tension, it's clear; we can have whatever we want, now. Our eyes have been opened by a new tree and a new fruit. The old world had gone as far as it could; but in the new, the eternal opens out before human beings, once again.

At this crucial moment, let's be clear; the source of human Rights is not to be found in institutions; politicians; or manifestoes. No; it's in a blazing Concept, Supernal and Spiritual.

This Perfections seems to be the final purpose of man; a creature with *such enormous potential* for the Beautiful and the Good.

God-willing, he will wake up and realize who he really is; and remake the world in the spirit of his true Image and Likeness.

All The World's A Stage

One man believes the Democrats will solve America's problems, that climate change is the world's greatest threat, and that social progress is paramount; while another believes Republicans trump Democrats, Liberals can't be trusted, and that radical extremists are an omnipresent omniscient threat. (The only thing they both agree on is that we are in constant danger.)

The training for this mindset starts early, as children are taught practically from the cradle that the pilgrims were thanksgiving heroes (and not litigious cranks), that America is a nation of destiny (and therefore cannot be undermined by the dark forces), and that one ought to trust implicitly the politicians and the press (despite their mercurial perfidy).

This early training, that is: worldview sculpting, is largely responsible for the irrepressible hope Americans have that next set of rascal politicians will be the ones to save the day. And of course, one must belong to one of these parties. You are an American, aren't you?

In this way, the public is groomed from birth to serve a sociopolitical dichotomy engineered to generalize individuals, with Big Media bearing the lion's share of the edge rounding.

Depending on your Network Programming, with CNN and FOX being the chief dialectical agents, you will more or less receive a worldview created for you by Big Money (which hides behind Big Media), thinking wholeheartedly you are objectively informed, and that by tuning in you are being a responsible citizen.

This sort of sincerity is exactly what is being played upon, as the Media trades on the trust its forebears enjoyed, exerting such authority wantonly, and brutalizing its audience with ubiquitous installments of quotidian fear.

Meanwhile, Big Media skirts you past crucial knowledge pertaining to the real Globalist threat, through the looking glass, down the rabbit hole, past Alice and the Cheshire Cat, Blitzer O'Reilly and Wolf Shepherd, and back again, none the wiser.

But don't look too closely at the Foundations that corrupt through charity; the Food Giant that began by making poison; the Space Program that appears to be installing Control Grid infrastructure; the Science Insiders turned worldview promulgators; and let's not forget those other worldview formulators, the Ad Agencies/Temptation Brigades.

But why cover these dreary things when you can harp endlessly on Slick Hilly's emails?

Indeed, the American politician and his corresponding outlet exist in a scripted vacuum, where fireworks fly and fingers rise in a transfixing drama, with cardboard heroes and villains, where the stakes are real but the play is staged.

The Perception Machine paints over reality and fact in a pure confidence game, doubling down by charading constantly (thus daring you to unmask it), and doing so by employing blatant word repetition downloads.

Here is a recent example:

Extremist, Extremist, Extremist. ISIS, ISIS, ISIS. I.S., Extremist, Radical, Rebel. Now multiply that times Infinity.

But perhaps I haven't been fair to FOX and CNN. After all, their blues and reds are so pleasing to the eye, and the cascading stars that shoot across the screen look like liberty personified! If only America didn't lock up such a high percentage of its citizens; and if only it didn't invade countries fighting terrorism, meanwhile allying itself with the barbarous likes of Saudi Arabia and Qatar, perhaps I too could sink back into my easy chair and zone out to the soothing flicker rate.

But this is just the problem: Big Media crafts a scripted dream of liberty that no longer coincides with reality, even as it bombards with seemingly infinite information/crises from all over the world.

All the world's problems are now our problems, and all the world must soon converge to save itself from the problems caused by going Global in the first place. The climactic moment appears to be approaching, and the climax of the networked drama seems eerily close to reaching its zenith.

With Media having taught the players how to act in the national drama, the curtain is now parting, and the stage is set for international tragedy.

To paraphrase Shakespeare: all the world's a stage … and all the world is staged.

What it all seems to boil down to is that as the powers-that-be have become exceedingly corrupt, so too has the once venerable fourth estate. Working together, in fact merging and overlapping, they appear to be promulgating a universal narrative, twisting perception via all-encompassing Media, to create easily controllable, homogeneous clones.

The mind and reason itself are the targets. Peer pressure is used to coerce consensus. And television is the medium channeling the haunting of minds.

I don't know about you, but my television's days are numbered.

Our Lady As Humanity's Symble Of Aspiration

"A great sign appeared in heaven: a woman clothed with the sun, with the moon under her feet and a crown of twelve stars on her head. And She was with child."

Her hands are clasped in prayer, and Her head tilts slightly forward. Around Her are the rays of the sun, and the ribbon 'round her waste means she is with child. You see, She is always brining Christ into the world.

This is the image of Our Lady of Guadalupe, and it is the same as the mystical image from Revelation. To this day, humble and invincible, it's somehow still stamped on Juan Diego's cactus-fiber tilma. Scientists have no idea how the fabric holds the image; or why it didn't crumble centuries ago; or how the Virgin's eyes somehow reflect characters from the room where the image was first presented. The facts are inscrutable, and science cannot penetrate them, nor explain them away.

The story behind the image goes something like this. In 1531, the Virgin Mary appeared to one Juan Diego, and, long story short, gave him a set of summer flowers still blooming in winter; in order to prove to the Bishop that She was really appearing to him. After Diego gave the flowers to the Bishop, wrapped in his tilma, there was an additional surprise! Upon it was the image of Our Lady, dressed in the traditional fare of a Mexican peasant. She called Diego "my little one", speaking like a local; like a close relation.

All this was happening as Calvin, Luther, and myriad European people were defecting from the Church. Meanwhile, the Mexican people were discovering a treasure; they had a Heavenly Mother who loved them! The millions of conversions to the Church after Her apparition roughly equals the millions of defections in Europe; a true Renaissance of culture, especially considering the barbarous practices of certain Aztecs.

Fast-forward to the present. For so many reasons, the meaning of Our Lady, Her symbolic importance, Her role in the Church, and Her role in history, are misunderstood. This writer was actually accused of idolatry by a Protestant, recently, for posting the aforementioned image on Social Media. I felt like replying, "There are more things in heaven and earth, Horatio, than are dreamed of in your philosophy". After all, Hamlet's Horatio was visiting him, at that time; come from Wittenberg; where Martin Luther was teaching! Hamlet is big with religious subtext; and, I assert, buried deep in the text is the suggestion that formerly Catholic England may just be guilty of marrying its divine Spouse's less-worthy brother.

If I had to explain to someone, who didn't understand, why I, and so many other Christians, venerate the Virgin Mary, I would make these points. First, as Christ is the new Adam, so She is the new Eve. With Her continuous "yes" to the Father, She cancelled out Eve's betrayal. Second, She has been venerated since the early times by Christians for being "the God-bearer". It's really just common sense to understand that the One who bears God must be beyond reproach; singular; and full of Grace. Third, She has been appearing throughout history, assisting, admonishing, and vanquishing the enemy.

Unfortunately, many Christians have no knowledge of Christian history, and their explorations go no further than sacred scripture.

In the Gospel of Luke, the author makes a subtle connection between Mary and the Ark of the Covenant. Like the Ark, Mary is the one on Whom the Glory of the Lord descended. She contained the Manna, The Staff, and the Word. She became the mystic link between earth and Heaven; and nobody else could have done what She did, because Our Lady alone was pre-sanctified. If She had said no to the angel, there would have been no future for the human race.

When I see the Virgin on stained glass, in sculpture, or on canvas, I see the symbol for the whole Church; because She represents each one of us. She first satisfied the Divine desire to dwell within human tabernacles, as in the early times. Afterwards, this honor became available to all; but even though each Christian is a tabernacle, there is still but one Holy Ark; which in one sense represents all Divine/Christian synthesis; and in another, the very heights of supernatural union.

But even with all Her supernatural privileges, notice her humility and gentleness; Her piety, which is remembered throughout ages in the poetry of the Magnificat ("My soul magnifies the Lord"); Her grace which, lavishly bestowed on Her, She preserved in the midst of an impure world; and Her charm, which drew the Holy of Holies from the center of Heaven.

Note Her proximity to miracles in scripture; from the Incarnation and the wedding at Cana, to the pre-sanctification of the Baptist, the Redemption, and the descent of the Holy Spirit.

Her life on earth was but one continuous miracle. Who can say what mystic flights occurred, and what absorption into the Trinity She experienced, during Her nine months of Divine Maternity; what romance, what ardor was contained in that holy "yes"? Perhaps this is why the Ave Maria is so mystically beautiful; as it seems to contain all mankind's yearning for the Eternal, and the hush just before the accomplished Incarnation. Within it is our story, as our Heroine, like a more beautiful Molly Bloom, presses Her hands to Her breast; and with Her mind racing, and Her "heart going like mad", says, "And yes, I said yes, I will Yes".

Reflections On Divine Mercy

It's an article of the Faith to believe that God is infinite, transcendent, and composed of Persons.

We take all this for granted today, but the fact is the majority of ancient religions have held God to be either part of nature or impersonal. But even if they thought Him personal, those persons tended towards being fabulous, and/or conniving. For many peoples, God was simply the ruler of a particular place. And many of these particular deities got swept up into enormous pantheons, like that of Rome. Others seem to once have been the God of everything, like Pan or Demeter, but later had to share power with other unfortunate all-powerful entities (hence the constant competition between gods).

Jewish monotheism was a revolution in respect to all this. The entire world was polytheistic, and the Roman world, which controlled the known world, was really only playing lip-service to its religion. The rites were performed by priests who were holier than the gods themselves. The incense was offered, the sacrifice was made, and that was the end of it. Hopefully the god was appeased, but could the person possibly be? This is the environment the Merciful Savior entered into, adding to and improving the theology of the Jews, in a time when no-one else would dare make such exclusive claims about a Deity.

Today, these claims have lost their revolutionary savor. But it still makes my mind reel when I try and ponder that God is Infinite, Trine and yet One.

In His many attempts at giving God a face, man has made Him a monster, a chimera, and even a swan, but it has never made Him Merciful.

We could never have conceived He would go to the extent of Incarnating, to communicate Himself; gestating within a tiny little body; becoming a helpless infant; made dependent, hungry, and unable to walk.

C.S. Lewis compared the Incarnation to a surprise attack on an enemy beachhead. Here the King shows up unannounced, in occupied territory; born not in a palace (where the devil would certainly be looking for Him), but in a squalid stable. He shows up inpromptu to test His priests, and they ask Him for His credentials. His response? Who I Am should be obvious to you. Wow.

And He is killed by His priests, the people of His covenant, and by His Roman children. On the face of it, it's a tragedy. But in the classical sense, it's also a romance, because there is a wedding at the end.

Divine Mercy bridges the gap between God and human beings; human beings that begin as little embryos, but end up as kings of an eternal Kingdom. Mercy is what designs the way to bridge the gap, after first desiring it; for It yearns to share Its glory. As such, It has gone to the extent of dying to give Divine Life; and even breaking Itself into Bread, to feed the souls of men. Looking at that Bread on the altar, sometimes I just shake my head, unable to fathom the extent to which God has gone to lift up human beings.

Divine Mercy is Holy. Three Times Holy. Unapproachable, but entirely reachable. Infinite, but made imminent. Unfathomable in the way It places itself at the mercy of human beings. Astonishing, paradoxical, graceful and noble, and adorably humble. Who could have guessed this would be what the Face of God would look like? the Face that He would turn to us?

So many today look upon the Church with contempt, thinking it exists just to play the spoiler. I like to tell people that the purpose of the Church is to turn men into living tabernacles; to be one thing with God,

Himself. To be sons of God! Not even the angels can say this! Essentially, the Church exists to turn men into gods. And to teach mankind how to love. This is exactly what attracted the Greeks and Romans of the first century, because they saw men being transformed in front of their eyes, and they marveled at it.

The essence of Divine Mercy can be seen in the extent to which God went to turn human beings into others like Himself. He would stop at nothing. Literally, nothing. And I'm convinced that even this total Self-donation is but the very beginning of the knowledge that is to come, in the Life that is to come, which will be the justification for so much abasement on behalf of the sublime Merciful Savior.

May He be praised forever! Amen.

With A Crown Of Twelve Stars

Let There Be Light

Veritas Gazette

Indie Band "The Walkmen" Are A Hidden Gem

The Walkmen are one of those rare bands that has somehow stayed beneath the radar, despite evident talent and strong songwriting craftsmanship. Passionate, lyrical, and melodic, their music suits a variety of moods; and the styles vary as well, shifting effortlessly from one song to the next.

This review will focus mainly on the albums "Lisbon" and "You and Me". "Lisbon", the more recent of the two, begins with three very strong tracks. All three songs are tinged with a streak of surf-rock, although I wouldn't describe that style as defining them. Take the lead track, "Juveniles", for example. "Juveniles" rocks a major-key riff, to a tongue-in-cheek vocal delivery; in a mid-tempo number, with a drumbeat that almost skips along. Its climax delivers the stirring line, "You're one of us, or one of them", sung with satirical glee by front-man Hamilton Leithauser, to the crashing of symbols, and ascending Rickenbacker scales. Truly a strong opener.

Following this is "Angela Surf City", an up-tempo number, which doubles-down on drums, as percussionist Matt Barrick rips the joint to pieces. The band masterfully ebbs back and forth between tension and release, like wave following wave; investing the song with passion, as its subject is addressed with the quip, "You took the high road; I couldn't find you, up there". "Angela" pops and crackles with intensity; I dare you not to jump up and down when you listen to it.

And then there is "Blue as your blood". "Blood" is undeniably influenced by the Spanish ballad (which should come as no surprise, given its lyric, "Spanish is the language of your tongue"). But what does come as a surprise, is that hidden deep within it is a surf-rock vibe. This hidden quality is intangible, yet somehow the band has made it tactile. Not everyone will be able to appreciate its Iberian Mysticism, but with this song, the Walkmen have somehow transposed the idiom of the Spanish ballad into the form of the "three minute pop song"; and without straying into "Knights in white satin" territory, too.

Other highlights include the mournful, yet still up-tempo and romantic, "Woe is me"; the sparse, Italian sounding, "While I Shovel the Snow"; the minor to major-key shifting, "Lisbon"; and the floating "Torch Song", which seems to drift by on a Venetian gondola. If there is any criticism of the album, it's that not all the tracks are equally strong. But that's not a huge drawback, considering this is pretty much par for the course. What is good here is great, and what is fine is just alright.

Shifting, now, to "You and Me", this album is more meditative than "Lisbon", although not without rocking numbers. "Canadian Girl" has to be the highlight. It's a deceptively simple pop song, that picks up steam as it goes along, building on a bouncy melody that is just a joy to listen to. "Canadian Girl" really takes off in the middle-eight, with a surprise burst of brass, that saturates the track with elegiac stateliness. Disappearing before the third verse, the horns ride out the track to the end, then vanish again, in favor of guitarist Paul Maroon's textured, bell-like echo.

"I Lost You" is gloriously gloomy. With stately drums, that remind somewhat of the Beatles' "I Want To Hold Your Hand", "I Lost You" builds and builds before exploding in the climax, with a cry of passion. Leithauser really lets loose on "You", belting out the chorus like a new Bono, but with more grit in his delivery.

"Red Moon" you might remember from the show "Breaking Bad". It's a slight departure from their usual guitar-driven mode, as the band opts instead for a base that rests on the piano. (I hope that sentence wasn't *too* confusing...) "Red Moon" sees the brass return once again, entering warmly with the start of the first verse. Another "love, loss, and lament" themed ballad, "Moon" showcases the legendary line, "Darkness is all around me tonight; you shine like the steel on my knife" (a couplet I think any poet would covet). This sort of dark romance is a mode of the soul more common to the European tradition; thus it's refreshing to see it coming, for once, from the continent.

Other recommended tracks include the climactically crashing, "On The Water"; "Long Time Ahead Of Us ", which features a slow-burning, low octave brass blaze in the middle-eight; and "Four Provinces", which has a notably intricate rhythm. Drawbacks include the use of echo, and occasionally abrasive guitar tones; plus a few tracks which don't seem to go anywhere. Beyond these complaints, "You and Me" is an exceptional album. Like anything else, you take the good with the bad; and there is lots to like here.

Naturally, the Walkmen have much more material. I would recommend checking out songs from other albums, like "The Rat", "Heaven" and "Dreamboat", as well. But concerning the two albums reviewed here, the band has created a strong body of music, and they've done it using fairly simple arrangements. Phil Specter's Wall of Sound this is not (although, please, do yourself a favor and get the Specter produced "All Things Must Pass"; a George Harrison classic). Nevertheless, the Walkmen still manage to makes beautiful and powerful music; exhibiting restraint, melodically; but before you know it, they've turned the dial up to eleven.

Be the first among your friends to pick this up; they'll be impressed at your Indie creds, and you won't be sorry you shelled out a few bucks for such a good find.

Book "How To Cook A Wolf" A Classic Culinary Compendium

A wise man always eat well" Chinese Proverb

"How To Cook A Wolf", by MFK Fisher, is a hidden gem. Written during WW2, "Wolf" deftly derides the "war machine", and the "slick magazine[s]" that ridiculously promote "balanced meals", at the expense of the individual; so that they are the same from "schools and prisons", to the "Arizona Biltmore". According to Fisher, our "Democratic Diet" is routinized, because, "What kills the least number with the most ease is the chosen way".

Clearly, Fisher has an activist's spirit. But the idea of the book is not so much to rail against the powers that be, as to cook the wolf at the door, and eat it (after making it taste delicious, of course).

As such, Fisher provides tips, recipes, and advice for living during times of shortages; but the recipes and tips in the book are great for any age; and the prose is so compelling and hilarious, that it makes for a great read, even if you're not that into cooking.

Here are a few tips I gleaned from "Wolf".

1) Add Sherry if you see an opening

2) Try pigeon and rabbit. On rabbit, Fisher writes, It "has always been associated with good fellowship" and "the jolly reconciliation of man and his fate".

3) Use water sparingly while cooking vegetables, so it will not absorb the vitamins.

4) When cooking eggs, wash them in cold water first, if you wish to hard-boil them. This way they won't crack.

5) Fish and eggs are rare in wartime, and during times of shortages, because the flesh is delicate. Fish is always best fresh, and with as little sauce added as possible (If fish is fresh it will not smell very fishy. A fishy smell tells you the fish is aging). And by the way, did you know you can use the oil from a tuna-can to make French dressing?

6) Soap can be made at home, with lye, water and fat. (This tip is from the section on how to make toiletry items at home, during a shortage. She also includes a good recipe for mouthwash).

7) Stuff your oven full of dishes to cook, and your stove-top with things to boil in pots, in order to save money. And use the by-products of your soups and vegetable-boils for bases.

8) "Liquor by the case is generally about 10% less expensive than [it is] by the bottle." (lol)

Aren't these wonderful tips?

Fisher's recipes are also very provocative. Here is one of her recommendations for after-dinner fare. "If you have supped well, for instance on ham baked with apples and sweet potatoes and a green salad, you will probably agree that the best possible ending to such a savorous meal is a bowl of walnuts that have been roasted in their shells in the hot oven while you ate. Coffee is fine with them, but a glass of port is even better...".

Then there is "War Cake", or "Cake from nothing", which includes such common ingredients as "shortening", "sugar", "cinnamon", "chopped raisins", and "baking soda". Of this cake, Fisher writes, "I remember liking it so much that I dreamed about it at night".

In the section, "How to Drink to the Wolf", we are provided with this stirring recipe, which Fisher calls, the "Half-and-half cocktail". I will relate it verbatim. "1/2 cup dry vermouth. 1/2 cup sherry. 1/2 lemon. Ice. Dash of bitters if desired." Excuse me for a moment, while I make one of these.

Her recipe for Beef Tartare is simple, and can be accomplished without much fuss. Beyond the beef, "egg" is required, plus "olive oil, parsley, chives, basil, salt and pepper". After the recipe (as with the dozens of others she provides), there are instructions included for cooking it.

Last of all, in the chapter titled, "How to rise like new bread", the author gives a variety of ways of making it, even in the most difficult times. For example, her recipe for "Hot Loaf", uses potato as a base, instead of flour. Of cooking bread, Fisher exclaims, there is nothing that will "leave you emptier of bad thoughts than this homely ceremony...".

There are too many good tips and recipes, in "Wolf", to do the book justice, here. And furthermore, how could I adequately convey the author's sly wit, and dry sense of humor? It is really a neat thing to read her dry quotes on war; as they pop up in such unexpected places as her post-war recipe edits. For instance, "Quote now that the war is over hahaha unquote, I would add three times that much fat to the pot". (The joke being that the war never really ends.) And then there are the references to her grandmother, who constantly chides her ancient friends to get over their war-rationing mentalities. (This makes me think of 1984.)

And even though she writes, "my mind says "next" [now, rather] than "last"", when looking for an adjective to modify "war" (in her less innocent, post-war edits), Fisher's "Wolf" is primarily concerned with serving said wolf up with delicious verve, rather than lamenting that he first knocked and growled. In this way, it is a hearty reminder to focus on the good that we have, rather than on the evils of the age.

Do yourself a favor and get "How to cook a wolf"; it might just save your life one day. But it will certainly serve your palate, and enliven your culinary sensibilities. Bon Appetit!

10 Great Tips For Writing Well Polished Prose

Let's face it, the English language is vast and complicated. We speak it and write with it, sometimes well and sometimes poorly; but how often do we reflect on it's usage? With this in mind, I've put together a few helpful tips to reduce common errors. These ten tips come in the form of rules and advice. I hope they will be helpful to you (and that they will make you laugh, as well!).

1) Onto vs. on to. The following sentence is incorrect. "Hang onto your hat." This might be correct if you were standing on it, and someone advised you (for some unknown reason) to cling to it as well. A thing can be placed "onto your shoulders", or you can be "onto someone", but otherwise, be sure to use the other form. And now, we're on to some more common mistakes.

2) Into vs. in to. If in the sentence you're using, you can drop the "in", and it still makes sense, then use "in to". Here is an example of what not to write. "Hey, dude, after we get refreshments, let's go into the movie." Clearly, the dude who is speaking doesn't mean he and his friend will be blending with the film. What's missing here is the infinitive, "to see". A better sentence would read, "let's go in to see the movie".

Use "into" to describe transformations and entrances, as in this sentence. "I must turn into the driveway before twelve, or risk turning into a pumpkin. By the way, when we go in to dinner, please leave Sally alone; she's just not that into you."

3) Irony. It's really not all that ironic people misuse this word, because it seems they never knew what it meant to begin with! It would be ironic to misuse irony if the speaker were, say, a school marm, or a perpetual corrector. True irony consists in saying one thing and meaning another. Such as, "Wow, chef, that is the best fly I've ever eaten; and the soup wasn't half bad, either."

Likewise, an ironic statement plays against expectation; as when it turns out that the storied frog is really a prince, or the article on grammar you're reading makes you laugh despite expectation.

4) Decimated. If you think this means literally, "One out of every ten men was killed", give yourself a pat on the back. To decimate means, "to destroy in part". So the next time someone tells you they feel decimated, smile and say, "So you're at 90%? That's great! I, on the other hand..."

5) Which vs. That. If a comma is involved, use "which". That's all I have to say about that.

6) When and how to use "that". For the most part, you can use it or not, it's up to you. But there are a few exceptions. Take this sentence, for example. "Petunia thinks your sweater stinks and Michelle does too." Now, does this mean "Petunia thinks Michelle stinks", or "Michelle thinks the sweater stinks, also"? A better way to render it would be to state things this way. "Petunia thinks that your sweater stinks, and Michelle does, too." Watch those sentence constructions! Many times they can be unintentionally hilarious.

7) You can end a sentence with a preposition, *and* split an infinitive. For example, "If we don't start to bravely balance our books, we just might go under." "Bravely" splits the simple infinitive, "to balance", and "under" pre-positions (er, post-positions?) the word "go". It's the twenty-first century, folks, and this is just common usage, now. Feel free to write angry letters. My address is: 101 Grammar is Flexible St., Sea of Tranquility, The Moon, 86753-09.

8) Must one always place a noun before a verb? "Says who?!"

9) There is no such thing as "chomping at the bit", champ. Just sayin'.

10) If you "draw a blank", it's "easier said than done" to use a phrase that's "cutting edge". So be careful, lest your audience be "bored to tears". In other words, innovate!

  With a few tips, and just a little bit of thought, you can make your writing more precise; so why not do it? Otherwise, you might find yourself telling jokes you weren't aware of, like the one about the cook who went into dinner, and found the soup to be too hot. There has to be a balance with language, because one can't be too strict, but we also have to preserve meaning. With a little effort, one can learn about language all life long, yet enjoy the process, as well.

SPECTRE Review

SPECTRE, the new Bond film starring Daniel Craig and directed by Sam Mendes, continues and perhaps completes the rebooted Bond narrative, which began with the 2006 production of Casino Royale. Symbolized by the octopus, which features prominently in the gorgeous opening credits, this shadowy international organization, whose tentacles reach into everything from terrorism to the green movement, has been a Bond staple for decades; but in this film is exposed in a way never seen before.

SPECTRE continues the new tradition of Bond applying a more visceral approach to intelligence work, albeit enacted in a more measured manner (keeping the body count to a minimum). This seems in keeping with Mendes' most graceful camera work, and the wearing of Tom Ford's top flight suits, which somehow remain nicely pressed, even after Bond flies a wingless airplane into two menacing SUVs.

The acting is solid, with Ralph Fiennes and Christopher Waltz, among others, turning in top notch performances. But the locations are what make the film, with Mendes supplying surpassing elegance and a calm confidence to the direction, steadying the helm well amidst the havoc and mayhem he's devised for his international set pieces.

Alongside the main narrative of Bond vs. SPECTRE, a parallel subplot emerges, as once again MI-6 and the "00" programs are under scrutiny by meddling bureaucrats. In a referendum on the efficacy of modern intelligence, these agencies are in danger of being shut down in favor of a draconian computer network which would eliminate personal privacy on a world wide scale. Once again, in an increasingly familiar move, Craig's Bond goes off- grid (causing his co-workers no shortage of distress), in a move that makes one nostalgic for the days when your nation's trusted assassin could just slip off in his requisite Aston Martin, without the chip in his arm alerting seventeen agencies.

SPECTRE is in many ways the quintessential Bond film, remaining true to the new style, while incorporating classic elements from the past. Both series fans and casual movie goers should find it thrilling in the main. If there is any criticism, it's that the film runs a bit long at two and half hours, and seems to jettison its dramatic stakes, concerning the fate of the entire free world; reducing them to a personal conflict between one villain and his protagonist. But that is a small qualm, considering the dashing excitement delivered by SPECTRE. No other franchise provides action and elegance on a scale like this. Here's hoping Daniel Craig comes back for a fifth film! (4/5 Stars)

Sacredness in Les Mis

Les Mis the musical and Les Mis the movie, by virtue of directed imagery, have been rendered two distinct entities. Though the lyrics of the musical are drenched in redemptive imagery, the stage has generally been left bare, for the mind to supply itself with scenery. The film version, however, surprisingly and overtly drapes its frames in Christian imagery; embracing crucifixes, crosses, convents, and sacred spaces.

The sacred and the profane, wild, revolutionary world, are starkly contrasted against each other: the desacralized world manifesting in revolutionaria and in the degraded masses; the sacred in redeemed characters. The fruits of both are represented: the anarchic and the wrathful versus the peaceful and the edifying; perpetual revolution versus ongoing redemption.

This review will concern itself more with analysis of symbols and imagery than with plot and dramatica. Even so, I feel the need to remark that the decision to have the actors perform song live lends humanity and realism and is much appreciated.

The opening scene rises up from the depths of an oceanic abyss towards a submerged French flag. Perhaps this signifies the French condition; tossed by tempestuous waves and drowned by the sound of sirens.

The camera then pans over a galley ship being hauled into a dry-dock by chained prisoners. As the camera descends, it swoops over the wings of a wooden angel, carved into the bow of the ship. This will be the first of many visual cues that alert the viewer to the sacred contained within the film's visual aesthetic.

Interestingly, ships feature several times in the film, specifically ships out of water and wrecked ships. Do these perhaps represent humanity, as fragile, damaged vessels, wounded by life?

Above the masses of prisoners who are hauling in the ships by ropes, standing on a ledge, is Javert, the inspector, who will pursue Jean Val Jean (heretofore referred to as JVJ), relentlessly. He is shown on high several times in the film, peering down upon humanity with severity.

As it turns out, JVJ is to be released on this day, but not before Javert requires him to lift an extremely heavy flagstaff attached to a sullied French flag in the water, like a Christ figure, on the way to Calvary.

JVJ ascends into the mountains, "from when comes our salvation;" and is framed against the backdrop of a cross on a pillar of stones; and beneath a brilliant full moon, symbol Our Lady. Ok, director Hooper, you have my attention.

JVJ wades through a sea of fallen humanity; is beaten and mistreated by children and adults; before collapsing on the doorstep of a Priest; who embraces him, even in his fallen and wretched estate.

JVJ makes off with the Priest's silver, like a new Judas, only to be captured by policia and returned to the Priest in his guilt; who defends JVJ, thus securing his immersion in Grace. Val Jean paces back and forth beside a horizontal crucified marble Jesus. The ceiling is crowned with stars. Exiting the Priest's domicile, JVJ passes through a courtyard filled with crosses, departing for a life of Catholic Christian charity and honor (as the Priest commends him to do).

Several years into the future, a montage of the bereft masses of humanity ensues, singing in chorus: "At the end of the day." The poor starving masses are sick with cholera. Their desperation is palpable; both internally and externally.

We advance to JVJ's factory, where the former criminal has made himself an honorable life, using the Priest's silver to put the poor to work. Fantine, mother of Cosette, is working alongside a series of cruel, obnoxious women; dressed in a delicate, feminine pink, compared with her dully clothed co-workers. She is like a flower beside various strands of darnel.

It is revealed in this scene that Fantine has a child. She is kicked out of the factory for this.

Javert has been pursuing JVJ doggedly, and they meet face to face in the factory, after Javert peers down upon him from on high. Val Jean hands him a Rosary. Since when has Hollywood ever felt the need to add sacred symbols to film without denigrating them? My jaw slackened. Immediately after this most Catholic of symbols is transferred, a cry arises from the street; a man is trapped beneath a cart beam; the weight of this cross shaped yoke is crushing him, and JVJ, the man of Grace, lifts it from him.

Javert recognizes Val Jean in this action, as if the lifting of the cross was his own personal Emmaus. This rescued man will later return in Les Mis to reciprocate help for JVJ in his moment of need; merciful reception is a recurring theme within the work.

Meanwhile, Fantine is most bereft. After losing her job, in fear of the future of her sick child, she wanders the streets of the desacralized, brutalizing world. She sells an heirloom and her hair; and like a feminine Sampson, proceeds to lose her virtue and strength. As she is being seduced to prostitution by a horde of sirens, to the tune of "Lovely Ladies," a demonic statue is flashed instantaneously.

A vista of ruined ships is presented before the eye. Fantine yields up her ship's treasure to a leering "Captain," but not with her heart contained within the action. After her patron leaves, she sings "I Dreamed a Dream."

"There was a time when love was blind

And the world was a song

And the song was exciting

There was a time

Then it all went wrong."

Souls who tend towards Grace mourn for their lost innocence.

A man assaults Fantine in the night, and Val Jean rescues her. She is now feverish. He lifts her into his arms like a child, and carries her to the safety of a convent to convalesce; she is tended to by nuns. Fantine gazes absently into a linen curtain, adorned with a large cross (death is the last cross; a just sentence and a last purification for fallen men).

Behind the veil, Fantine glimpses a phantom Cosette, angelic, reaching towards her through the cross. Who is behind this movie? She dies in the arms of JVJ, the bestower of Christ's largess and mercy, in ecstatic contemplation.

The contrast between the cold secular world and the comforting sacred one is most striking.

Javert, who is the omnipresent accuser, a Lucifer figure, appears in all his wrath, to impose the law (as JVJ has fled parole). I imagine Val Jean would have gone with Javert, save for the fact Fantine's daughter is entrusted to him. JVJ fights Javert off with a (cross?) beam, and plunges into salvific water, leaving Javert again on high: like the Prince of the power of the air. His prey is again snatched from him; removed by inscrutable movements of grace.

Now, Cosette appears in reality; unkempt and neglected, singing: "Castle on a cloud." Souls instinctively yearn after Heavenly imagery. She gazes up into a window at the image of a mother figure and sings: "There is a lady all in white." Is this Our Lady?

Through mysterious operations of Grace, Cosette is rescued from her cruel existence by JVJ. What began as a chance encounter with a Priest, has blossomed into a life of mercy sanctified by love of God. Though Val Jean was once bereft, a little seed of good-will planted in him has become a holy tree, branching out exponentially.

After liberating Cosette, JVJ discovers the ruefully ubiquitous Javert again in chase. He takes refuge in a convent. The sisters are singing the same song sung by the Priest at his initial moment of conversion; a signal that we are redeemed in merciful actions? Time is given to note the pacific beauty and order of the prayerful peace of the sisters en chapel; lit to the point of loveliness by candle-light. A foretaste of Heaven?

As Val-Jean peers down upon the Churchyard, we notice the rows of horizontal crosses, perhaps symbolizing the joining of Heaven and earth in the person of Jesus? Most Mysteriously, JVJ and Cosette are taken into the care of the man Val-Jean liberated from beneath the beam. Grace proceeds to further Graces.

A quick scene of Javert gazing blankly into a crucifix, and he is on the rooftops again, nimbly striding the edge. He sings, "And if they fall as Lucifer fell," while standing by the bust of a bird of prey/phoenix, symbol of the fall of Lucifer. This goes a long way in confirming my theory that Javert is a Lucifer prototype.

The camera ascends over a cross, crowning the roof's pinnacle, and then descends upon the Paris of unruly mobs of children, who sing, "Look down… here in the slums of Saint Michele." Michele is the French form of Michael, the ArcAngel responsible for driving Lucifer out of Heaven. Perhaps there is more to this revolution than meets the eye?

Phase two of the film is concerned with revolution, displaying the suffering, starving and sick masses converging in the streets; a desacralized wild mass; contrasted by the privileged, who dine adjacent to them. Javert, the accuser, is everywhere; seeking to hinder Grace, which he is not able to perceive; a child of the law and of wrath, as he is. He locates JVJ and Cosette in Paris.

Though Val-Jean is opposed continuously by Javert, invariably, his forced and hindered actions flower in the opposition; revived by mysterious movements of Grace.

They are forced to flee, but not before Marius and Cosette exchange meaningful glances; falling in love instantly; the way events obtain syncronicity only in the movies.

Meanwhile, revolutionaries of the June Rebellion, Marius included, gather in Café Musain (whose closest cognate is inspiration), to plan further post French revolution action. They thirst to shed their blood and youthful vigor for a wild dream of temporal glory; singing "Red and Black.

Red is the blood, and black is the death of revolutionaries.

Marius (read: Mary is) counters, singing: "The world can change in but one burst of light."

"Our lives don't count at all," counter the revolutionaries, with typical youthful bravado.

It is, of course, entirely up to us, whether they do or not.

Leaving the den of wild men, the camera frames a virginal Cosette, safely hidden within her room, a sealed fountain, against the backdrop of delicate flowers, symbolizing her lily purity. Her garment is woven with flowers. Bunches of blossoms hang outside her window, like ripe clusters of grapes.

Might this suggest a contrast between earlier scenes of lost innocence and human degradation?

Is this still a Hollywood film?

Bunches of lovely flowers halate Cosette as she emerges from her garden to greet Marius. Between them is the garden gate, guarding her lily white purity like an ArcAngel.

In harmony they sing "A heart full of love." Indeed.

Marius is followed, and Eponine, who is the daughter of the innkeeper JVJ rescued Cosette from, alerts the household with a cry. Fearing his cover is blown, Val-Jean gathers Cosette, and flees.

Special attention is made to JVJ packing the candle sticks the Priest gave him in the beginning. Perhaps they represent the phrase: "You are the light of the world." Candles are recurrent in Les Mis, especially in sacred spaces.

A montage of red. A red flag is waved by the revolutionaries. The revolutionary leader is adorned in a blood red coat. Javert is displayed wearing a French flag pendant, attached to his jacket by a swatch of red ribbon.

At the funeral of the people's leader, Lemarque, the rebels descend upon his casket's coach, hoisting their blood red flags. Javert is disguised within their ranks. His wrath is clearly omniscient.

Inverted flag-pyramids of black and gold sway in the wind, hanging from the halls of justice: symbols of Masonry; who proudly take credit for the French Revolution. Crosses with streamers flank the streets.

Shots and chaos ensue. "To the barricades!"

Child sized coffins are stacked in front of the makeshift barricade, presaging the tragic death of a child; and the grown children who are so misguided and sadly secularized, to the point of dying for a mad impromptu dream.

Outside the walls of the Church, our Mother, what is there for man to do but debate endlessly and foment strife?

Speaking of walls, what could the makeshift barricade represent but the paltry and artificial divisions erected between men, which incite them to war against each other, who are really brothers descended from one Adam? Divided men are not able to witness the humanity of their brothers. This is the object of barricades.

Above the coffins and barricade is a prominently displayed all-seeing eye; symbol of the mystery religions and Masonry. It is, in fact, displayed quite brazenly; just a bit to the left on the main building. The French Revolution is considered part of the Great Work of the Ages. The elite are guiding history from behind the scenes, and many see our times as being the crucial moment in the history of man.

Battle ensues at the barricade, and Eponine is slain by a stray bullet; expiring beneath a sign reading "mort;" French for death. In her last act, Eponine gives to Marius the note Cosette left to instruct Marius as to why she fled; she is thus freed from her constricting possessive love, and is liberated in death.

Marius seeks Cosette, thereby drawing JVJ behind the barricade, where he spares the life of Javert.

This is a grace which might have converted Javert, but instead polarizes him in his condition of wrathful creature; demonstrating how graces can change into condemnation when dismissed with ingratitude.

Upon over-hearing Marius sing his love for Cosette, JVJ is moved, and intones: "God on high," framed curiously beneath the Eye. Symbolism is seldom missing in this film!

Quickly after this song and its attachment to the Eye, bursts a clever quick shot of a soldier crouching with rifle in hand, beneath the eye. He whistles sharply, and the camera dashes left. Blink and you will miss it.

A battle at daylight.

Marius is shot and JVJ whisks him away; always a savior.

The rebellion is a disaster. The rebel leader is cornered in the café, shot, and hangs cryptically out the window, over the word Musain (inspiration); a blood red flag in his cold dead hand. The streets run red.

JVJ drags Marius through the sewers to safety. As Paul writes, "Jesus assumed the form of a servant," to redeem fallen men; leaving

117

glorious Heaven for our sakes. Val-Jean is completely covered in filth by his saving action; head to toe. And yet, Marius, who is unconscious, is unaware. How many men truly ponder what Jesus took upon His divine Person to secure Redemption? The pure one became "All sin" for our sakes.

Javert confronts JVJ in the street, but is impotent in his wrath; frozen by the demonstration of Val-Jean's total dedication to Graceful saving action. He can but gnash his teeth in fury, at defeat. What can he say? His whole life and purpose are overthrown by the salvific power of JVJ's annihilation in Mercy.

Glorious Mercy outshines the law like a star against a little lamplet.

Javert paces on the edge of a precipice, above salubrious fountains. He sings, "I am the law and the law is not mocked," before hurling his person over the edge. His entire life is a prelude to this moment. Pride goeth before the fall.

The waters Javert disappears into dissolve in painted images of angelic cherubs over Marius' hospital bed.

Alone in the Café Musain, Marius sings, "My friends, don't ask me what your sacrifice was for."

Marius brings Cosette to his family home, no longer a revolutionary, as Grace is now operating in his life. Marius and Cosette sing in unison, "Every day we will remember that night and the vow that we made."

Human romantic love, when balanced and proportionate, leads the lovers to the love of the divine One; Who is the highest goal of men, beyond the earth.

As JVJ confesses his past to Marius, a cross divides them. This overt imagery is a continual surprise.

As JVJ flees to leave the two free to marry, an enormous crucifix adorns the wall behind him.

Marius discovers JVJ saved him in the sewers, at his glorious wedding, and seeks him out of gratitude. JVJ is where? Where else? In a Cathedral.

A close-up of a crucifix and a dying Jean Val Jean.

"God on high, hear my prayer," ascending from this earthly abyss, to Thy throne, sings Val-Jean.

A sevenfold candelabra illuminates the chapel, symbolizing the sevenfold Spirit of God.

Cosette and Marius appear to comfort John, Valorous John; and he blesses them, laying his hands upon them like a Patriarch; as Fantine sings to him: representing how the good works we perform accompany us at the hour of death.

The angelic Cosette comforts her father in his last agony, as Marius proclaims: "Cosette, your father is a Saint."

"God in Heaven, look down on him in Mercy," is sung by Fantine.

This is "The story of one who turned from hating," Jean Val Jean.

"To love another person is to see the face of God:" all in chorus.

Love for Fantine and Cosette was Val-Jean's individual redemption.

The Priest who redeemed JVJ receives his soul on the threshold of life, within the Cathedral courtyard, enveloped by glorious candlelight.

Outside the Church walls, a closing scene unfolds: an enormous barricade where all the dead gather, waving red flags; singing "Tomorrow comes." They are a sea of tempestuous humanity; raging perennially; the blessed and the reprobates gathered together, like a final resurrection.

The timing of this movie is curious to me, as revolution rages in the world, and seems to presage increasingly greater turmoil. Hollywood

is expert at revelation of the method; and I surmise that we are boldly
presented here with our choice; as we stand, like Javert, on the precipice
of events, to either leap into the Arms of our Father, or plunge headlong
into the abyss of chaotic infernality.

Mind Control and Mysticism in the Bourne Identity

More and more I am simply blown away by the audacity of the elite. In films like Cabin In The Woods and The Hunger Games they are simply giving their plans away. Of course, it isn't like anybody notices. Once again, in the person of Jason Bourne, a segment of the plan is revealed. This time, the subject is mind control; a topic which tends to make people's heads spin.

Bourne is the archetypal super-soldier. One must sit patiently through the three films to glean this info, but he has volunteered for a program in the black-ops department, and has gotten more than he has bargained for. Tortured to the point of dissociation, Bourne is instructed to kill a hooded man in the lab, with no justification other than that it is necessary. This completes his mental snap, which is the object of the training.

Why the mind control? Super-soldiers cannot be allowed to remember their assignments; and they must be controllable, dispassionate; unfeeling.

The truth of matters is revealed slowly in Bourne.

We begin by viewing him in the water, submerged. This can be interpreted as a lustral cleansing. I do not think this is such a stretch, considering some of the later nomenclature. In lustral water, Bourne is born again, like a new Adam.

He is rescued by a merchant ship pilated by Italians (Roman Catholic?). As it turns out, Bourne has an implant with a bank signature. You see, the assassins are owned by the international bankers.

How did he wind up in this baptismal font? Simple, on a mission orchestrated by the intelligence agencies, Bourne's programming breaks down mid-hit. While on a ship contemplating assassination, the images of children upset his programming. Innocence is the precursor for Bourne's regeneration.
Cooincidentally, the alias Bourne is using for this hit is Kane.

Before entering the regenerating font, becoming Bourne again, Kane is wounded in the presence of innocents.

Of course, the fact that his programming is scrambled means Bourne could not function at all, but the point of this exercise is the exploration of mind control, not psychological theory.

A digression. There are different forms of mind control. There is the subtle mass manipulation of people by electronic media, whereby they are sucked into the television and hypnotized in accordance with their own will; and there is the less voluntary kind, whereby individuals are robbed of their freedom by a combination of deprivation, drugs, torture, and technology. These combined tactics play on the mind's ability to escape from reality, creating extra coping personalities, that can be accessed and programmed for missions.

These techniques have been employed in the occult world for generations, and have been tapped and refined by the elite in the fields of the military, entertainment, and government.

Back to Bourne. Knowing nothing of himself, he goes to the bank to check on the account number embedded into him. This ritual return to the source is symbolic of monarch programming. Monarch butterflies have genetic memory of their place of generation, and return there. Apparently, monarch mind control subjects pass the genes of programming onto the next generation; making them even more suggestible.

Bourne descends deep into the earth into the recesses of a Swiss bank. A banker tips off the intelligence agencies that he has arrived. Though still oblivious to his identity, Bourne now has a lot of cash, and many passports. He picks up a bright red bag at the bank, and stuffs it with diverse currency. The color red is significant in this film.

Bourne winds up in the US Consulate, where he finds Marie Kreutz, who is having a great deal of trouble with her papers. As surveillance is omnipresent, Bourne is soon discovered and harassed; but escapes with Marie.

Marie is Bourne's salvation. Look at the name! Marie Kreutz = Mary Cross in English. She drives a bright red auto. I have been pondering the significance of this color, and I think I know what it means: red is the color of blood: salvific blood; blood that is shed in redemption. I do not know why such symbols are displayed sub-rosa in Hollywood films.

Mary of the Cross sweeps the Man re-Bourne away from harm. They travel to Paris, the land of frivolity, where Bourne has a domicile under the name Kane. Kane? Really? Perhaps Bourne is the man of grace reborn, and Kane is the wicked one; his evil doppelganger.

The exploration of his personality continues, as Bourne examines his apartment; lovely but Spartan.

An assassin bursts in through the window. A tense and bloody struggle ensues, where Bourne uses his heart to overcome the superior firepower of the assassin. Faced with certain death, the assassin, named Castel, throws himself off the balcony. Why? The mind control assassin is programmed to self-destruct to avoid capture.

Bourne escapes with Marie by creating a diversion, and they escape.

On a side note, the mind control assassination program is named Treadstone. Treadstone? Hmm. This phrase brings to mind the Masons walking all over us.

Bourne surmises he is an assassin. He and Marie have a falling out, but remain together, and travel to her step-brother's house in the countryside to avoid capture.

The intelligence community is all over it. Having snapped an image of Bourne and Marie together in the car, they triangulate their probable position. Just try and hide from the all seeing eye!

Another assassin is sent after Bourne, who has superior position and firepower, but again Bourne uses his heart to surpass him. Before dying, and revealing the name of operation Treadstone, the assassin makes a curious statement: we always work alone. Whether mind control assassins, or mind controlled lone-gunmen, it is always thus.

In the Bourne series, several assassins are activated by cell phone. They are shown de-activated, dormant, until the trigger command is issued, which springs them to life; accessing the command center of their minds.

Furthermore, the intelligence handlers are shown attempting to access Bourne's programming over the telephone, using control commands. However, Bourne's neural circuitry is shattered like a glass hammer. It is revealed that agents compulsively return within a certain time-frame, in accordance with their programming.

It is a good thing this film is not about mind control!

The film ends with Bourne having a face to face with one the program directors, who informs him he is an asset who has cost the government a good deal of "hard-earned" cash.

Treadstone is nixed to avoid scrutiny. Enter Operation Blackbriar.

Beyond the visual pyrotechnics and visceral power of The Bourne Identity, is an exploration of the mechanics of mind control; wrapped into a mystical enigma. Perhaps Hollywood cannot help but explore the duality in personality that informs Bourne; but why explore mystical elements?

There is an obvious resurrection; a sordid past; a saving mother archetype; subtly sacred visual cues; a struggle of good versus evil; an underworld of nefarious and hellish characters; and mystical nomenclature in the names of the characters.

All of this makes the Bourne Identity into the prototypical mystery wrapped in enigma.

About The Author

Chris Veritas

ChrisVeritas.blogspot.com

Cleopatra

cleopatrapoem.blogspot.com

Let There Be Light

WithACrownOfTwelveStars.blogspot.com

Mind Control and Mysticism in the Bourne Identity
TheBourneIdentityreview.blogspot.com

Sacredness in Les Mis

LesMiserablesReview.blogspot.com

The Song Of Solomon Turned Into Poetry

MySongOfSolomon.blogspot.com

Ecclesiastes Turned Into Poetry

EcclesiastesPoem.blogspot.com

Off Rail Alliance

OffRailAlliance.blogspot.com

Esoteric Analysis of "I Pet Goat 2," Psy-Op Viral Video

iPetGoat2.blogspot.com

Movies, Music, Health, and Books

VeritasGazette.blogspot.com

The Book of Wisdom Turned Into Poetry

MyBookOfWisdom.blogspot.com

Quoth The Raven, "Veritas"

ChrisVeritas.blogspot.com

where good code goes and nobody knows

htmllimbo.blogspot.com

About me

Gender   MALE

Industry   Publishing

Occupation   poet/philosopher

Location   bolivia, nc, United States

Introduction   Member, Skull and Bones. Royal Society. Yale, 1922.

Interests   music, poetry, chess

Favorite Movies Casablanca. Casino Royalle

Favorite Music Radiohead. Mozart.

Favorite Books Everything That Rises Must Converge. Anna Karenina.

www.ingramcontent.com/pod-product-compliance
Lightning Source LLC
Chambersburg PA
CBHW070811240726
48654CB00007B/301